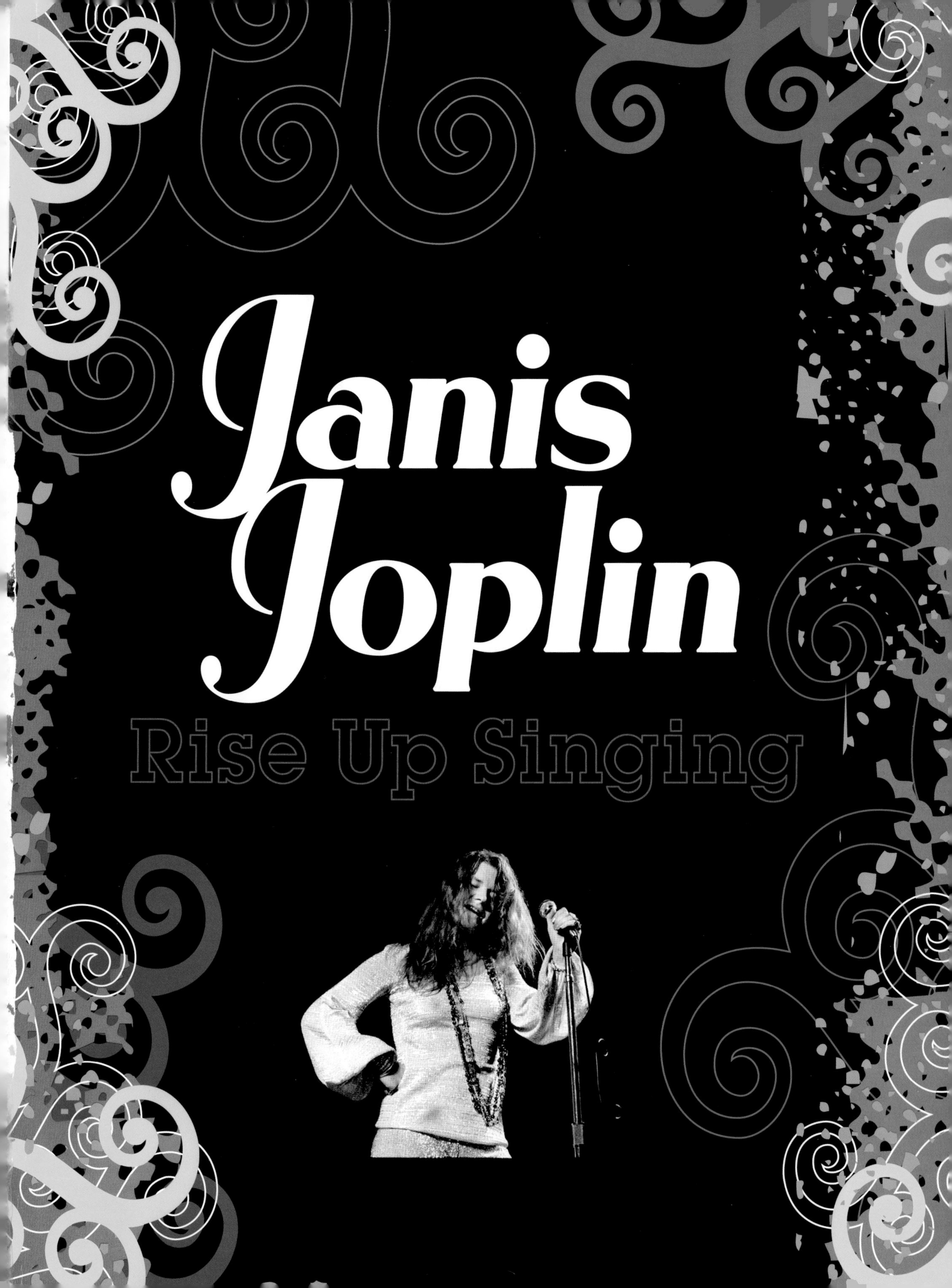
Janis Joplin
Rise Up Singing

Janis Joplin

Rise Up Singing

Ann Angel

Introduction by Sam Andrew

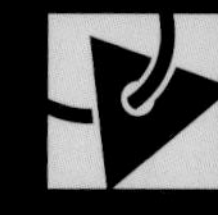

Amulet Books
New York

For Jeff—You always rock my world

Library of Congress Cataloging-in-Publication Data

Angel, Ann, 1952–
Janis Joplin : rise up singing / Ann Angel.
p. cm.
ISBN 978-0-8109-8349-6 (alk. paper)
1. Joplin, Janis—Juvenile literature. 2. Singers—United States—Biography—Juvenile literature. 3. Rock musicians—United States—Biography—Juvenile literature. I. Title.
ML3930.J65A83 2010
782.42166092—dc22
[B]
2010005558

Book design by Maria T. Middleton

Printed and bound in U.S.A.
10 9 8 7 6 5 4 3 2

ABRAMS
THE ART OF BOOKS SINCE 1949
115 West 18th Street
New York, NY 10011
www.abramsbooks.com

Contents

Introduction

Sam Andrew plays guitar while Janis sings. Band mate James Gurley is in the background. After playing together in Big Brother and the Holding Company and the Kozmic Blues, Janis and Sam remained friends.

Janis Joplin was my best friend. I played with her more nights and days than any other musician in her life. We were both obsessed with how to make the music better. When we drove home after playing, all we talked about was how to improve what we were doing. What an intro would do here, what a series of notes would do there, when the drummer should come in, how this song would be better than that song as a final tune.

Janis was the most powerful person I have ever known, and yet she was completely insecure at the same time. She was the Queen of the Scene and the chambermaid, simultaneously. It was always, "Hey, how was I? Do you think they liked it? I mean, it was all right, wasn't it? What do you think? Tell me. I want to know. You like me, don't you? You really like me, right? Don't just stand there—tell me what you think. Was I good? Did I do all right?"

From a person as talented as Janis was, such questions could be unnerving. Her talent was so obvious, but often she couldn't see it herself. People discount what they do best, because they think, "Well, hey, this is easy, anybody can do this, so what's so special?" Janis made me realize that what we do best, all of us, is natural to us, and easy to take for granted. This is completely understandable, and yet it is important for each of us to appreciate our natural gifts, and take pride in them.

We all like to pretend that we are above caring what others think of us, and that we can be indifferent to both praise and blame in our better moments, but alas, we often fall short. Janis was no exception. She may even have cared too much what people said about her. We were somewhere—New York, Cleveland, maybe even San Francisco—and a critic wrote, "Janis Joplin has true melisma in her singing." She had to look up "melisma" in the dictionary, where it was described as many different scale tones used over the same word in singing, a common vocal technique in Gospel or choir music. After she had learned what it meant, Janis didn't stop saying the word "melisma" for a week. That's the way she was about praise. She couldn't get enough of it.

Janis loved Ma Rainey, Bessie Smith, Victoria Spivey—real pioneers in blues, singing in an era (the 1920s) when it really counted to sing with feeling and power. You can hear their influence in Janis's singing. Janis herself showed the way for people like Joan Jett, Patti Smith, Fiona Apple, Pink, and Lady Gaga—each one exhibits some facet of that Janis character and style. She was vulnerable, powerful, super wide open, talented, and interesting in a kind of terrifying way.

Many writers wrote that when Janis died, it was somehow a suicide, or maybe even that the music industry had murdered her. This is all as untrue as it is completely beside the point. It's important to realize that Janis had more fun than ten people; she was always alive, completely energetic, funny—very funny—and strong. She was nobody's victim. It wasn't somehow ordained by fate that Janis should die so young. Her death was an accident. Janis had big appetites. If it was food, then she wanted to eat the most. If it was drink, then she, naturally, wanted to drink the most. If it was life and living, then she lived it, crackling with energy and cackling with laughter, wanting the most from every minute. There was electricity in the air when Janis was around, and I will always miss her.

Sam Andrew
Big Brother and the Holding Company
The Kozmic Blues

1

Spreading Her Wings

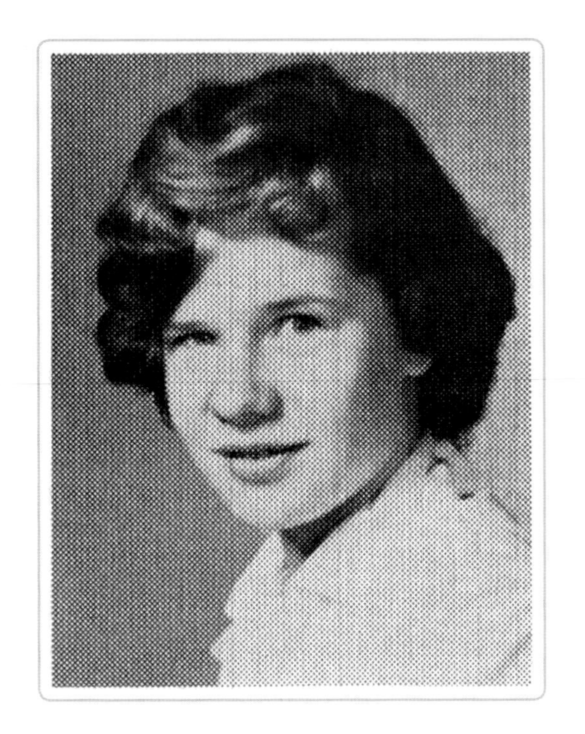

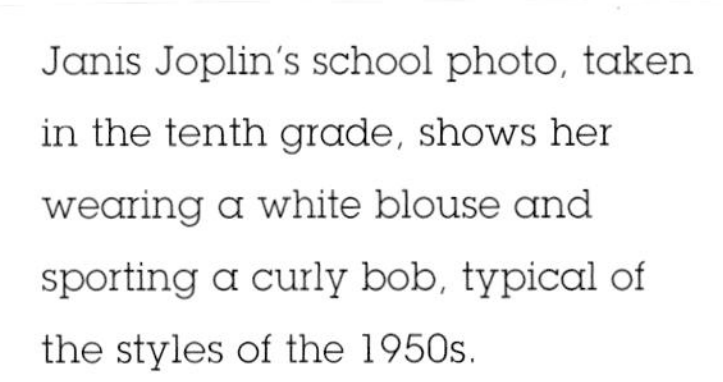

Janis Joplin's school photo, taken in the tenth grade, shows her wearing a white blouse and sporting a curly bob, typical of the styles of the 1950s.

The popular girls wore their hair short and perfectly curled, with tiny bows fastened at their temples. Their skirts swung demurely as they walked down the school halls. The round Peter Pan collars of their blouses were buttoned neatly and decorated with tasteful circle pins and pearl necklaces. The girls were pretty and petite, their soft, jingling southern laughs drawing smiles from teachers and from the boys who jostled for their attention.

Janis Joplin had only to look in the mirror to see frizzy brown waves of hair that refused to be tamed and a plump face spotted with acne. She was heavier than the other girls. Louder too. When *she* laughed, it came out as a cackle or a raspy, flat "hah!"

She was smart and well read, but brains weren't a ticket to popularity in Port Arthur, Texas, in the 1950s. Janis's classmates expected to graduate, marry their high school sweethearts, and settle down to raise families. The girls expected to stay at home, just as their mothers had. The boys expected to work for the oil refinery, the main business in town. Being smart wasn't as important as behaving like a good, churchgoing American.

This was a time when people thought a great deal about what it meant to be an American. Across the planet, the Soviet Union was growing in power and global influence

This yearbook photo shows Janis as a member of an extracurricular group, one of many she participated in, which included the Future Teachers of America, the Slide Rule Club, and the Glee Club. Janis is in the front row, on the far right.

under a system called Communism, in which property was owned in common rather than by individuals. People truly feared the spread of Communism and what it might mean to American ideals of democracy and self-reliance. Demonstrating the virtues of being American, whether by behaving as your neighbors behaved or just loving baseball and apple pie, was seen by some as a way of warding off the Communist threat. This was an era for fitting in.

Janis tried. She joined the Future Teachers of America, the staff of the school newspaper, and the art club.

RIGHT: Popular singer Pat Boone rehearses at the London Palladium in December 1956 for his first British television appearance. Boone sang ballads and love songs typical of the popular music the teens of Port Arthur preferred in the 1950s.

BELOW: Actress Debbie Reynolds swings from a rope outside the haymow of a barn on the MGM lot in Hollywood in 1958 as she continues her work on a movie called *The Mating Game*. Reynolds, a singer and actress, was a popular draw for many teens through the late 1950s and early '60s.

But all that joining didn't help much with the girls at her school. Janis was too loud, her clothes too dark, her opinions too strange. While "nice" girls listened to songs about chaste love sung by well-scrubbed stars such as Pat Boone and Debbie Reynolds, Janis liked black music—blues songs about hard work, loss, and pain. She spoke out in class in favor of integration, of having black and white children attend the same schools. In a place like Texas, where separate neighborhoods, schools, churches, and even public bathrooms were the norm for blacks and whites, Janis's opinion deepened the chasm between her and her classmates. For a while, two boys followed her around her all-white school, pitching pennies at her and calling her

Odetta performs at the New Orleans Jazz Festival in 1978. The singer, whose voice Janis emulated, loved folk music, blues, and jazz and first become popular in the 1950s.

RIGHT: Author Jack Kerouac laughs during a 1967 visit to the home of a friend in Lowell, Massachusetts. Part of the Beat scene, he wrote *On the Road*, which influenced Janis's own beatnik philosophy.

OPPOSITE: The Rainbow Bridge, which spans the Neches River, was a favorite haunt for Janis and the boys in her group. They would climb the steel structure and sit, legs dangling down from their perches as they sang and talked long into the night.

Drawing and painting offered Janis relief from loneliness, and her parents encouraged her talent. On Saturdays her father would drive her to nearby Pleasure Pier to paint the waves rising on Sabine Lake. Painting, Janis said, made her content, but it also kept her inside herself, turning her into a recluse.

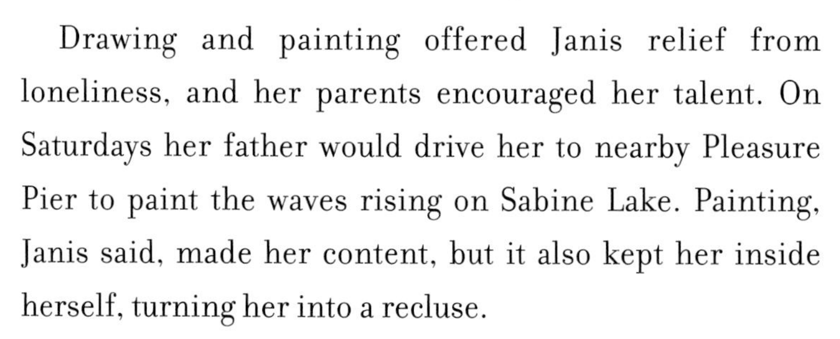

Janis gradually tired of both trying to fit in and hiding herself away. By the middle of her sophomore year, she started hanging out with a rougher crowd, dressing in the dark colors and short skirts of the more rebellious kids, teasing her hair, and talking tough.

She found friendship with five smart, artistic guys at school. This group considered themselves intellectuals. They introduced Janis to the literature of the Beats—writers Allen Ginsberg, Jack Kerouac, and William S. Burroughs. The Beats rejected conformity, like those circle pins and pearl necklaces and all they represented about doing what society expects of you. The Beats wrote of *really* experiencing the world without the barriers created by

middle-class comforts, of living rough, and of trying whatever life offered, drugs included. They stressed improving one's inner self and seeking soulful experiences rather than working for materialistic gain. In *On the Road*, his autobiographical novel about years of roaming the United States, Jack Kerouac proclaimed, "The only people for me are the mad ones, the ones who are mad to live, mad to talk, mad to be saved."

For a girl who struggled with rules, the Beats' ideas about personal freedom and rejecting conformity were very appealing, as was their embrace of a vast world of experiences beyond small-town life. Janis began to dream of leaving Port Arthur, spinning plans in long nights of drinking beer with the guys at an old coast guard station or climbing on the Rainbow Bridge over the Neches River. Janis could sometimes be seen up there, singing along to some old folk or blues song, her legs dangling over the water.

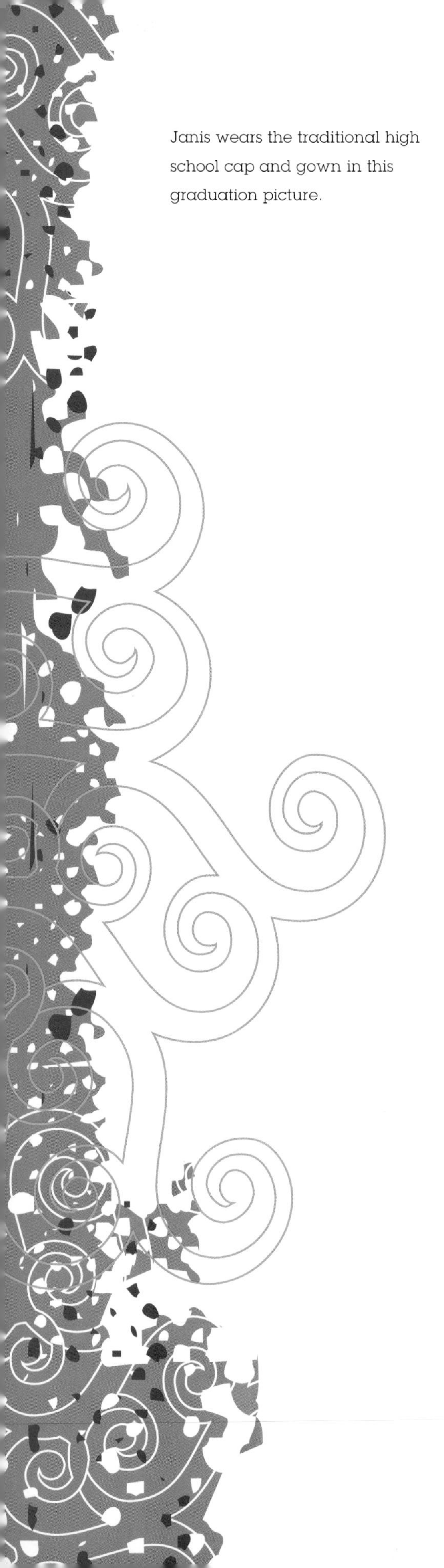

Janis wears the traditional high school cap and gown in this graduation picture.

Good girls hung out with just one boy—a steady boyfriend—not with groups of guys. Girls who hung out with several boys quickly got a reputation for being "easy," even if the boys were just friends. The school called Janis's mother in to talk about getting Janis to be "average." Parents warned their daughters to stay away from her, but they needn't have bothered: Most of the girls shunned her on their own.

The guys couldn't protect Janis from the disapproving looks and comments, or from the disdain her cackling laugh drew as it echoed down the halls of her high school. Sometimes, when that echo died out, Janis could hear kids slam their lockers and mutter "pig" as she walked past.

But there was no silencing Janis now. If anything, she stepped up her brash behavior. By senior year, it was a source of pride not to fit in. Still, school was torture.

At sixteen, Janis had almost all the credits she needed to graduate from high school, but she was biding her time. She wanted to escape Port Arthur, even if only to the nearby community college her mother encouraged her to attend. In reality, Janis hoped the community college would be a stepping-stone to Austin, a big Texas city known for its great art and music scene.

Janis attended her senior year part time. Many nights she could be found sketching at the Sage Coffeehouse, a Port Arthur "beatnik" hangout where her paintings hung on the walls. She sold a few paintings there and sometimes sang folk songs in exchange for tips she used as spending money.

Music was important to Janis and her friends, and folk music, with its lyrics of protest, spoke to them particularly—as did jazz, a favorite of the Beats for its improvisation and roots in black culture, which was outside the white mainstream. On weekends Janis and the guys would drive around, their territory expanding farther and farther from home, drinking beer and searching radio stations until they found one that offered the improvisational heat of jazz or the smoky tones of blues, Janis's own favorite.

Janis loved those nights when they'd all pile into a car and drive, listening to the radio or traveling across the border to Louisiana to catch live swamp blues, a lighter, laid-back form of the music popular along the northern Gulf Coast.

Sometimes they'd all sing along to the radio. Singing drew Janis out in a way painting couldn't. It made her want to talk more, to become more of the naturally flowing-out sort of person she felt she was instead of "a hold-it-and-be-quiet type."

During those nights on those car rides, Janis realized she could reach the vocal power of her favorite singers:

Bessie Smith, the Empress of the Blues; or Huddie Ledbetter, known as Lead Belly; or the folk singer Odetta. She'd sing along with Odetta to "Motherless Child." Then she'd get all Texas with her twang and keep harmony on "The Midnight Special" with Lead Belly and his twelve-string guitar named Stella. With her eyes closed, Janis would let her voice merge with the pain and misery of Bessie belting out the lyrics to "A Good Man Is Hard to Find."

Oh, how Janis knew the pain of being alone. Her voice carried the weight of longing as she imagined a life without a white picket fence, babies, or a man to love and call her own, the life that seemed promised to those pretty girls in pins and swinging skirts. She ached to be loved like that and to fit in. But when she was riding in the back of that car, feeling the Louisiana heat on her skin and smelling the earthy swamp breezes as they blew through the open windows and tangled in her hair, the world seemed big and mysterious. She'd close her eyes and imagine being anywhere but there.

Sometimes the guys would stop singing for a minute and just listen to the way Janis's voice could be light and then heavy, like a chime and a cymbal all at once. She pushed out misery and love, heartache and struggle. They'd hear Janis matching Bessie's voice note for note. It was on a night like this that Janis opened her eyes, saw the guys listening to her and admiring the music that came out of her a like a prayer, and announced, "I can sing." And they agreed.

Man, could she ever sing! The voice they heard in the backseat of the car would become one of the most distinctive voices of a generation, the voice of a new kind of music, the voice of the first queen of rock.

ABOVE: Janis loved to listen to the music of Bessie Smith, shown in this 1924 photo. Janis was so moved by Bessie's influence that, after learning Bessie had died penniless, she contributed to pay for a headstone on Bessie's grave.

LEFT: Huddie "Lead Belly" Ledbetter, a singer of blues and spirituals, named his twelve-string guitar Stella. Janis was influenced by his music.

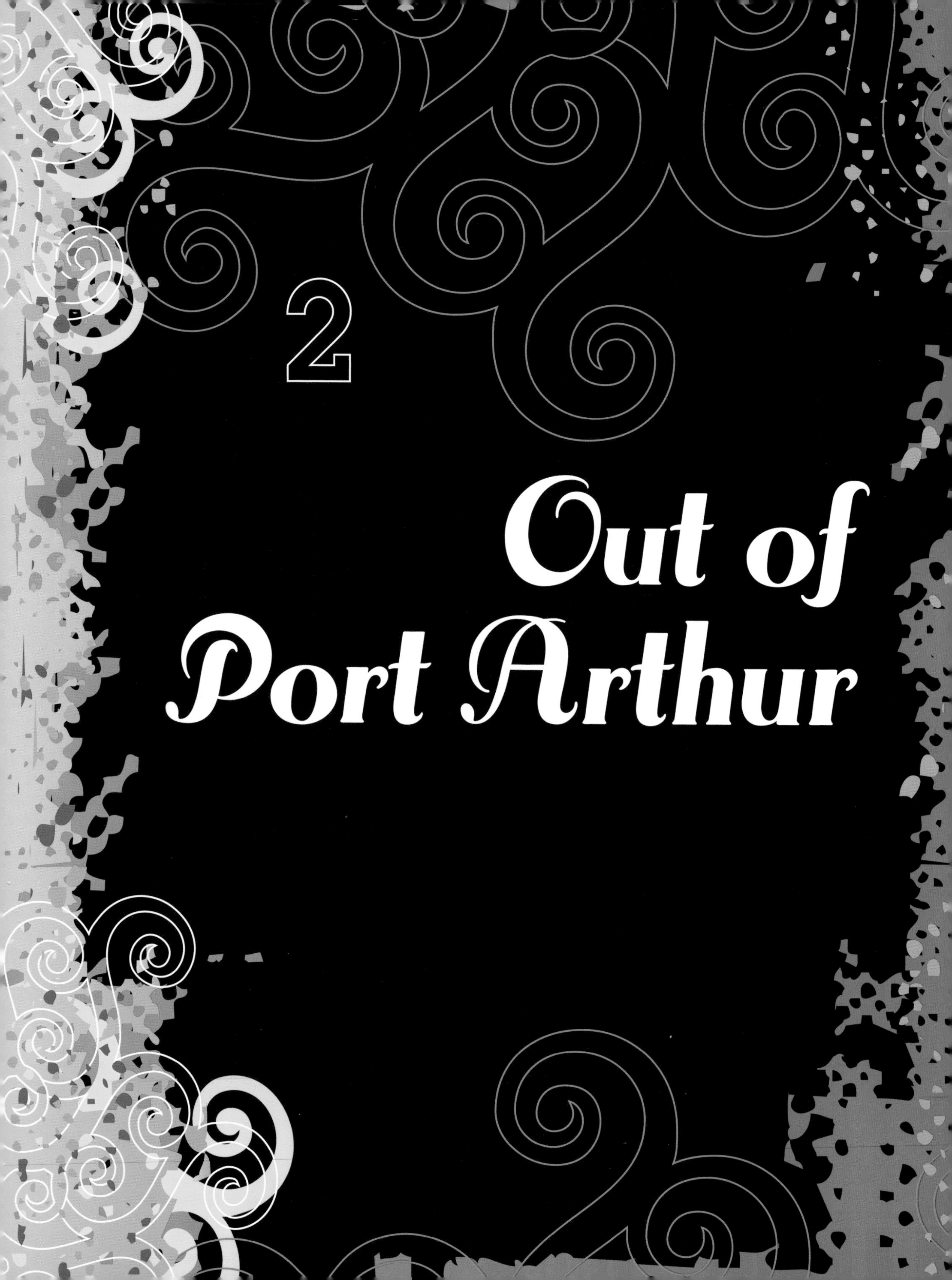

2

Out of Port Arthur

This undated photo shows a young Janis, most likely standing before her house, with her doll.

For most of her childhood, Janis Lyn Joplin was Seth and Dorothy Joplin's bright and pretty little girl in ruffled dresses and blonde curls. She was born on January 19, 1943. Her parents doted on her, encouraging her to develop a love of music. They purchased an upright piano when she was six, and Dorothy taught Janis to play.

Janis's father was a well-educated man with an engineering degree who worked at the large oil refinery in Port Arthur. He saw talent and intelligence in his oldest daughter, but also recognized that she was hard on herself and struggled to stand out as the best, recalling, "She went to church, sang in the choir and glee club, and painted. She was an artist, a good one. But she quit because she didn't think she would be as good as she wanted."

Janis sings with the First Christian Church youth choir. She is in the second row, second from the left.

Janis appears in the Tyrell Elementary School operetta. In this photo of the entire cast, Janis is in the first row, third from the right.

It was Dorothy's parenting style to include Janis and her younger siblings, Laura and Michael, in all conversations. As she explained, "We wanted them to voice their opinions and ideas about everything."

This cultivated a strong will in Janis, which she demonstrated even as a small child. She once sat at the supper table until bedtime rather than eat her hated turnips. And she refused to give up thumb sucking, even if it meant not being allowed to listen to a favorite radio show.

At school, Janis struggled with the strictures of the classroom routine. She asked too many questions, chatted with friends, and failed to get her work done on time. She often received poor marks in following directions and respecting others. Still, many of her teachers were fond of the lively, intelligent girl and found outlets for her creativity. Janis's beloved junior high school journalism teacher, Miss Robyn, gave Janis poor marks in citizenship but assigned the young artist, who was often caught doodling in class, the plum job of illustrating the school literary magazine.

By the time she was seventeen, school had lost much of its appeal for Janis, and she had begun her jaunts with her group of guy friends across the Texas-Louisiana border to sip beer and listen to music at roadhouses such as Buster's, Big Oak, Lou Ann's, and Shady Rest. Her parents began to really worry about their headstrong daughter.

It was one of these trips that stirred up real trouble at home. Janis's parents gave her permission to use the car to spend the night at the house of Karleen Bennett, one of her best—and few—girl friends. In reality, Janis had gathered three of her guy friends to drive down to New Orleans for the weekend. There, Janis was in a minor traffic accident, and the police realized the underage teen had crossed state lines with a group of overage boys. According to friend Jim

OPPOSITE: A smiling Janis wears a cap and gown for her ninth-grade graduation.

Langdon, who was along for this adventure, it was pretty scary. "They were talking the Mann Act," he said, referring to the law that made it a felony to transport a woman across state lines for "immoral purposes." The three boys could have landed in prison. "And the trip was all her idea!" Langdon exclaimed.

When the police called Janis's parents, her mother explained that Janis and the boys were just good friends. The police put Janis on a bus home but left the boys to hitchhike back to Port Arthur. Although Janis's mother had kept calm while talking to the police, both parents were becoming uncertain of how to handle the problems Janis brought on herself. But, as her sister, Laura, recalled, "Janis wouldn't accept the limits they set for her and she wasn't good at setting her own limits."

Janis's parents worried about her reputation and character. But more troubling was her appetite for risk. They worried she'd end up hurt or dead.

Stories of Janis's adventure in Louisiana spread like fire among the high school gossips, sealing her reputation as a social outcast and "loose" girl. A double standard existed then, as it still does, so while the boys were "just being boys," Janis was labeled "promiscuous."

Despite his worries, Janis's father seemed to understand her frustration with the rigid rules of behavior, particularly for young women. He called it the "Saturday Night Swindle," in that you could work hard all week and live a good and kind life but still end up unhappy, or poor, or unpopular and lonely. But he also saw fighting the rules as a losing battle. If Janis took on the town's hypocrites and phonies, she would be the one to pay in rejection and isolation. He didn't believe rebelling was worth the price.

By the time graduation came, Janis was desperate to

leave Port Arthur. She believed that "anyone with ambition like me leaves as soon as they can or they're taken over, repressed, and put down." She dreamed of making a career with her painting.

At first, Janis's escape, along with that of many of her group, was to Lamar State College of Technology in Beaumont, only an hour's drive from Port Arthur. Janis registered for art classes and moved into the dorms in the fall of 1960.

Living away from home for the first time, seventeen-year-old Janis basked in freedom and independence. Despite cruel gossip from the same teens that had ostracized Janis in high school—a crowd that also attended Lamar—she found her own tight-knit group of friends.

Some days she'd gather her friends, which included members of the old Port Arthur gang, and head to the nearby Paragon Drive-In. There, they would share a fifty-cent gallon of beer while watching movie after movie.

When they had a free day, Janis and her friends would run off to Houston, a big city ninety miles away, and hang out at the Purple Onion Coffeeshop. Janis told her sister about one of these escapades: She and her friend Karleen were pulled over for speeding and, with only moments to spare, managed to hide a bottle of red wine they'd been drinking.

3

Looking for Love

It didn't take long for Janis to decide that life at Lamar College wasn't much different from life in Port Arthur. It was the same small-town thinking: People weren't questioning the status quo; they were embracing it. At Lamar, she could be certain she would never experience the wider world the Beats promised.

Before her first semester ended, and at her mother's urging, she decided to return home and attend Port Arthur Business College to learn keypunching, a way of storing payroll, bookkeeping, and other data before computers were common. Janis hoped this skill would be her ticket to a job—and a life—farther from home. Determined to move on as quickly as possible, she passed a necessary skill-level test after just four months of training and withdrew from the college.

OPPOSITE: Janis, about seventeen here, signed this photo of herself playing guitar for her parents.

Her parents agreed that she should look for a job outside of Texas, hoping that she would be happier and not so restless away from the negative influences of old friends. Soon Janis was headed to Los Angeles, to live under the watchful eyes of her mother's sisters, Barbara and Mimi.

Janis got a job as a keypunch operator for the telephone company in California and lived in an artist's shack behind her aunt Mimi's house. Keeping mostly to herself, she happily painted late into the night, using oils and canvases that Mimi's husband, Harry, also a painter, kept stored in the shed. Before long, however, her nine-to-five job proved tedious. Bored and restless, she longed to explore the world and to *really* experience life as the Beats had. She was ready to live on her own, even if it meant struggling to make ends meet.

One day on the bus home from work, Janis struck up a conversation with a guy who was traveling to Venice, a beach community west of Los Angeles. Impulsively, she skipped her stop and continued on with him. It was worth the trip; Janis found a place where she belonged.

Venice had been the dream of a nineteenth-century entrepreneur who built it as a resort and amusement park, modeled on the canals and palaces of Venice, Italy. Though once a popular tourist destination, the resort had closed and the surrounding community had fallen on hard times. By the 1950s it was a center for beatnik culture. Artists, musicians, and writers, attracted by the cheap rents and quaint architecture, moved in and transformed the area. They opened coffeehouses, art galleries, and bookstores; they staged readings, performances, and exhibitions. Creativity, freedom of expression, and pansexuality were celebrated parts of everyday life—as were drugs and alcohol, which were seen as portals to heightened experience and deeper understanding.

Mother & Daddy

Janis

Janis found a ramshackle place she could afford on her own and settled in. Inspired and fueled by the seemingly nonstop creativity surrounding her, she resumed painting and singing. She sometimes spontaneously performed for friends at the Gas House coffee shop and art gallery, where she first heard about a similar scene in San Francisco's North Beach neighborhood.

On a lark, Janis traveled up to North Beach, hitchhiking just as her hero Jack Kerouac had done in *On the Road*. There, she befriended artist Dave Archer, then the doorman for the Fox and Hound coffeehouse. She showed up dressed in Levi's, a blue work shirt, and a sheepskin vest and smoking a cigar. "I don't remember the whole conversation, but I remember her . . . with that cigar in her jaw," Archer wrote later. "She said, 'I hear you hire *sangers?*'" Struck by the strange pronunciation of "singers," Archer asked Janis where she was from. "Port Arthur, Texas, but you don't want to know about it," she responded. That night, she sang the country song "Silver Threads and Golden Needles" for the crowd.

Struggling to support herself in California, Janis returned to Port Arthur in December 1961. She swaggered into town, seemingly eager to shock and impress everyone with her newfound, over-the-top California ways. She wore a World War II bomber jacket turned sheepskin side out and greeted one friend, Powell St. John, with the sexual come-on "Doesn't anybody around here ball, man?" When he responded no, her voice grew loud. "I want to turn everybody on to that!"

Her "flamboyance, that awesome braggadocio in her carriage and speech, so shattered their senses—unhinged them, really—that they were quite incapable of suspecting so much as the slightest exaggeration," explained a friend, who believed Janis's aggressiveness was in part an act, perhaps put on, as it had been in the past, for shock value and to mask insecurity.

As Janis quickly discovered, she was not the only one from Port Arthur to have changed. Her high school girl friends were beginning to marry and to talk gleefully of houses and children. Obviously on a different path, Janis wondered what kept her from being part of a couple. She admitted her conflict, announcing, "I want to want the white house with the picket fence covered with climbing roses, but I just don't."

She reenrolled at Lamar College for the spring semester, commuting back and forth to school from home, though life with her parents felt increasingly limited. Many of her guy friends had moved away, and in the summer of 1962 she, too, decided to leave, following a few of them to Austin and the University of Texas.

In this May 2007 photo, the sun begins to set over an oil refinery in Port Arthur, Texas. The derricks and storage tanks are typical of the oil-town landscape.

OPPOSITE: Janis Joplin joined the Waller Creek Boys—Lanny Wiggins (playing guitar) and Powell St. John (holding a harmonica)—for Wednesday-night folk-sings while in Austin.

Even in a large, diverse city like Austin, Janis's over-the-top behavior and radical opinions quickly drew attention. The *Summer Texan*, a school newspaper, published a profile of her a month after she arrived on campus. It began, "She goes barefooted when she feels like it, wears Levi's to class because they're more comfortable, and carries her Autoharp with her everywhere she goes. She leads a life that is enviously unrestrained."

Austin was known for its strong music scene. It seemed that every restaurant and club offered up blues, country, or jazz. Janis and two musician friends, Powell St. John and Lanny Wiggins, billing themselves as the Waller Creek Boys, began performing bluegrass, country, and folk music at local coffeehouses and house parties. The trio also frequently performed at a university hangout called the Eleventh Door and at Threadgill's, a local bar with a reputation among truckers and students for the best live performances in the area. Janis gained a lifelong friend in Kenneth Threadgill, who encouraged her music, and a devoted following among his customers, who admired her as a singer with "a certain spontaneity and gusto."

Despite her musical success, Janis still found herself an object of ridicule. In the fall, as part of a University of Texas fund-raising event to name "the ugliest man on campus," she was nominated. Though she would later treat the insult as a joke, it cut deep; Janis cared a lot about her appearance and remained deeply self-conscious about her weight and blemished skin. The nomination was one more reminder that ideal southern beauty—and femininity—eluded her. She prided herself on being "one of the guys" only to hate herself for the very same reason. Shortly after, she wrote to her parents about the incident, asking what right others had to be so cruel.

Janis bragged to friends about her sexual escapades in California, but it's possible that her first actual sexual relationship was with Powell, who fell head over heels for his spirited friend. Though he loved and accepted her for the complex person she was, their romance was short-lived. Janis longed for a boyfriend, but at the same time, said she wasn't interested enough to continue the relationship. As she told Powell, "I do what I do because it feels good, man." A little later she would date Bill Killeen, the editor of a campus humor magazine called the *Ranger.*

Neither relationship kept Janis from flirting with other people. Always hungry for affection, she compulsively sought attention from both men and women. Friends speculate that she had her first lesbian experiences in college. She didn't speak openly about her affairs with women, and in an era when homosexuality and bisexuality were stigmatized, she may not have felt that she could; however, the intensity of her interactions with certain women indicates that some of them may have been more than friends. (In particular, she and her friend Juli Paul were known for crazed, drunken fights that they sometimes carried into the streets.) In the years to come, Janis would be more open to friends and lovers about her bisexuality, although in the course of her life, she had many more relationships with men than with women.

Janis and her friends at the University of Texas spent most of their time hanging out in a rundown off-campus apartment complex nicknamed the Ghetto. A gathering place for campus radicals and freethinkers, it was a bastion of uninhibited behavior and outrageous parties. In a time of political and social unrest—it was the height of the civil rights movement and the cold war, and the country was preparing for war in Vietnam—the Ghetto offered students a context in which to meet to discuss social and political change, as well as to drink and experiment with drugs.

It was Janis who first brought pot into the fold. "She had smoked a few joints in high school, but it is well known by all of her friends that she never really liked grass. . . . Bringing it into the Ghetto was to impress people with the hipness she'd acquired in Venice," said Myra Friedman, who would later become Janis's publicist and beloved friend.

One night in late 1962, Chet Helms, a former University of Texas student, visited Austin from San Francisco, where

Concert promoter Chet Helms, who convinced Janis to try out as a singer for the band Big Brother and the Holding Company, stands with Bill Graham, another major influence on the San Francisco music scene. Helms, with long hair and glasses, stands to the left of Graham.

he worked as a music promoter and club manager. After hearing Janis sing at Threadgill's, he told her that if she wanted to come west again, she would find an enthusiastic audience in San Francisco. It didn't take much convincing. Janis willingly gave up her studies and, in January 1963, hitchhiked with Helms to California, this time with the dream of making it as a singer.

Once back in San Francisco, Janis worked at a series of odd jobs to make ends meet and learned to play the guitar so that she wouldn't have to pay a musician to back her. She returned to the Fox and Hound, now called Coffee and Confusion, and asked for a gig. She got a regular one singing folk music. Musicians at Coffee and Confusion earned just two or three dollars a performance, but they were allowed to pass the hat for tips. For Janis the hat would always fill, and the attention and applause proved as much of a high as that offered by any drug.

A fan offered Janis a free place to live, a basement apartment that she would share with a new friend and kindred spirit Linda Gottfried. They spent their days making art, playing music, and writing poetry, and their nights over shared dinners of SpaghettiOs and Fudgsicles. Like kids, they covered the walls, the floor, and the window ledge of the place with ink drawings.

Janis, now age twenty, began drinking more heavily. She was living the life she had dreamed of, yet gradually losing control. Drunk, she hurt her leg trying to climb onto a Vespa and missed the chance to sing at the San Francisco State Music Festival, an opportunity to perform for a larger audience that she would have been thrilled to have.

She drifted from small gig to small gig before moving, in early 1964, to New York City. She wanted to see Greenwich Village and figured she could make some money as a keypunch operator and perform at local clubs. In New York, she landed in a hotel that was a favorite of drug users. The newest and most popular drug was methedrine, or methamphetamine, a stimulant that was both legal and plentiful at the time. Known as meth or speed on the street, it gives users heightened energy. In all likelihood, Janis shot up for the first time in New York. By August 1964, when she purchased a yellow Morris Minor convertible with her earnings and drove cross-country back to San Francisco, her drug use had become more frequent.

According to her sister, Laura, "The longer [Janis] stayed in California, the more committed she became to the Beat focus on living in the present. . . . She consumed alcohol flamboyantly. She equated drunkenness with personal spontaneity because it temporarily freed people from social restraints. With the artistic community, she sampled other drugs for their potential to enhance the unbridled freedom she sought."

By 1965 Janis was in love with a speed freak named Peter deBlanc. Her speed use increased alarmingly along with his, and soon she was strung out—most likely injecting herself several times a day—malnourished, and sleep deprived. She weighed less than ninety pounds.

Speed was pervasive in the artistic circles in which Janis traveled: It was easy to get and it was cheap. Though there was little available information about it, some doctors even touted it as a viable treatment for heroin addiction (a false claim for which they were later arrested). While Janis was under the influence, "Life looked brighter, sounds seemed louder, and [Janis] felt more creative." Laura speculated that her sister, like many of her contemporaries, may have begun to use heroin around this time to come down from the highs she was experiencing on speed.

Quickly hitting rock bottom, Janis tried to sign herself into a hospital as a psychiatric patient but was rejected because she wasn't perceived as mentally ill. Then deBlanc, to whom she'd become engaged, was hospitalized for speed-induced psychosis. After he was released several weeks later, he helped Janis, who was frightened and messed up, to raise enough money for a bus ticket home to Texas. Drugs had scared her. They had overpowered her creativity and almost killed her and her boyfriend. She left San Francisco in May 1965 for Port Arthur, vowing to straighten herself out and to plan her wedding.

Janis kicked her speed habit at home while waiting for deBlanc to join her. As part of her effort to take control of her life, she did a dramatic about-face. She gave up her sheepskin jacket and jeans for conservative, long-sleeved dresses that would hide her needle tracks. She pulled her wild hair, a symbol of her sexual freedom, up into a smooth chignon, and she seemed to adopt the traditional lifestyle she had rejected for so long. In fact, her dress and behavior

became so staid that she could have been mistaken for a secretary or a schoolteacher.

That fall, as part of her recovery, she began seeing a psychiatric social worker, Bernard Giarratano. She enrolled in summer school at Lamar, took a "poise" class to develop a more feminine posture, learned to play golf, and joined her family for swimming at the country club. For a while, she even refused to drink. "My parents," recalled Laura, "were sort of holding their breath."

Janis admitted to Giarratano that in California she had pursued the lifestyle she thought was necessary to succeed in the music world. She'd been into more drugs than just speed: quaaludes, which sedated in an almost hypnotic way; heroin, a highly addictive narcotic that promised a rush of euphoria followed by drowsiness; and Demerol, a narcotic pain reliever. She was attracted to drugs that numbed her and smoothed out her anxiety about herself and how she was perceived. Though she demanded almost constant attention—with her loud, often crude public behavior and nonconformist points of view—she hungered for affection and acceptance. Deep down, she wanted everyone to love her.

Now, with the drugs kicked, Janis was determined to fit into life in Port Arthur. She was responsible and attentive to her schoolwork, and professed that she was looking forward to getting married and becoming a wife and mother, just like the girls she used to go to school with.

Though deBlanc visited once and wrote often while she was away, it gradually became clear that he was seeing other women and didn't plan to return to Port Arthur. The marriage was off, and Janis began dating a sociology major at Lamar. Even as she settled into life back home, she couldn't help but hope for "something interesting to happen."

She continued to sing and play for friends, and eventually agreed to play at the Half Way House in Beaumont for Thanksgiving. (After hearing her there, newspaper columnist and friend Jim Langdon called her "the best blues singer in the country.") She also began making frequent visits to Austin, where she sang and played at a few clubs, including Sand Mountain, the Eleventh Door, and Threadgill's. In May, she was featured on a blues bill at the Texas Union Auditorium. Before long, singing offers came from Beaumont and then Houston, and by that time Janis's parents were very worried about her return to music.

Myra Friedman, who grew up in the same generation, explained, "This was not a time when a father or mother would say, 'My daughter, my son, the rock star.' You wanted to say, 'My daughter, the sociologist.'" Why a sociologist? It was a proper career, one that indicated a person had obtained a solid education and would be a stable, upright member of the community.

By the summer of 1966, Janis was certain that her career was in music. She returned to Austin and told her parents that she planned to stay there. In reality, she was already considering a move back to California. Her old friend Chet Helms had called and talked to her about auditioning with a San Francisco rock band, Big Brother and the Holding Company. Janis had been clean for twelve months and was confident she could withstand the drug culture on the West Coast.

Though friends discouraged her from leaving Texas, suggesting she stay in Austin to develop her voice, a mutual friend of hers and Helms's convinced her to leave, promising her a place to stay in San Francisco when she arrived. In the end, Janis left for California without telling her parents. For the time being, she had overcome her demons and the urge to sing was too great to ignore.

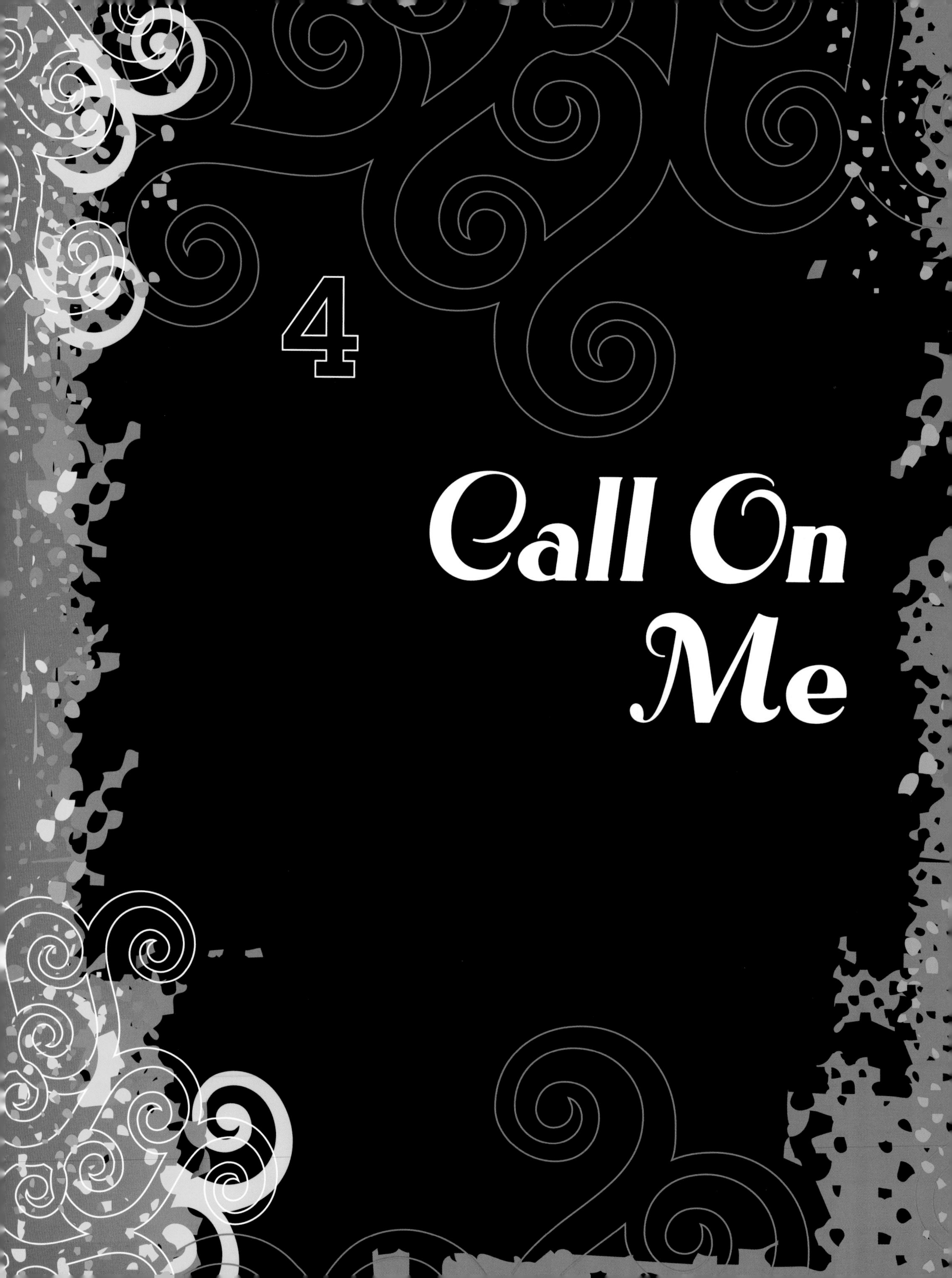

4 Call On Me

A young hippie walks by the intersection of Haight and Ashbury in San Francisco. Even after Janis gained some fame with Big Brother and the Holding Company, she enjoyed walking these streets and hanging out with the people she met.

The scene in San Francisco had changed while Janis was away. By June 1966, the neighborhood of Haight-Ashbury was a mecca for young "hippies"—a term coined by the media and derived from the Beat slang word "hip," meaning "cool." They flocked there for the cheap rents and established bohemian scene, seeking the personal freedom and rich experiences promised by the Beats.

Usually jobless and broke, but happy in the belief that they were living a better life than their parents, hippies, or flower children as they were called, preached the beauty of free love, peace and harmony among all races and creeds, and liberation from the bourgeois trappings of middle-class life. Creating ever-shifting families among themselves, they lived communally, crashing together in shabby, rundown apartments or abandoned buildings.

Their unconventional way of life was reflected in their colorful dress: Their clothes were often purchased secondhand and remade, embroidered, or embellished with feathers and beads. Both women and men grew their hair long, adorned themselves in strings of beads and rows of bangles, and celebrated—with their look—a lifestyle that was the antithesis of the one touted by the establishment.

Members of the rock group Jefferson Airplane are shown in 1966. At top right is vocalist Grace Slick. From left are Marty Balin, Jorma Kaukonen, Paul Kantner, Spencer Dryden, and Jack Casady. Jefferson Airplane was one of the first bands to come out of the psychedelic music scene in San Francisco.

And where there were hippies, there were drugs, more and more of them. LSD (lysergic acid diethylamide), or acid, the newest one on the scene, was among the most popular. A hallucinogen that alters perceptions, inciting colorful visions and blissed-out feelings, it was believed to open the mind to alternate realities, and to give users heightened awareness and deeper understanding. Legal—possession didn't become a misdemeanor until October 1966—and so cheap it was almost free, it had become intrinsic to the culture, and especially to the music of the time.

By the mid-1960s, folk and early blues had given way to psychedelic rock, a style of music characterized by the use of feedback, electronics, and intense volume. Wanting to create a musical parallel for the sensory experience of an acid trip, bands such as the Grateful Dead, Country Joe and the Fish, and Jefferson Airplane literally plugged in. They experimented wildly, trusting that their music and drugs would take them to higher levels of creativity. As Janis's sister, Laura, explained, "Few were then questioning the reliance on drugs in our society. Few were asking why drugs were needed. In those days, drugs were the new discovery. Who dared question the new shaman?"

Although Janis had met musicians Peter Albin and Sam Andrew before, she was reserved when she walked into her audition for their band, Big Brother and the Holding Company, known for their loud "freak rock" music. Other band members included James Gurley, who would be deemed the "father of psychedelic guitar," and drummer Dave Getz. Sam Andrew had encouraged Janis to try out. Though he believed the band had "produced some of the greatest psychedelic guitar solos of all-time," he felt they needed "a singer who could match the band's instrumental energies."

OPPOSITE: This Avalon Ballroom poster, from one of Big Brother's early concerts, is one of the first posed photos of Janis with the band. She was considered then simply one of the group and was not highlighted as the band's star singer.

OVERLEAF: Big Brother poses on a tractor for publicity photos, 1967, Woodacre, California. From left to right are Janis, James Gurley, Sam Andrew, David Getz (standing in front of the tractor), and Peter Albin.

Janis blew them away. Dave Getz recalled that, while she didn't look the part—pimply and shy, she was dressed in light cotton clothes better suited to summertime in Austin—"I knew she was absolutely incredible." The band made her their lead singer because, as Getz explained, "whether you liked her or not, you could tell that she was very extreme and unusual—a phenomenon."

Feeling guilty that she had left Texas without telling her parents, Janis wrote them a letter on June 6 apologizing but adding, "I really do think there's an awfully good chance I won't blow it this time." And sure enough, four days later, and only six days after her return to San Francisco, she was onstage with Big Brother. By the time the group appeared at the famed Avalon Ballroom, a key venue in the evolution of psychedelic rock, Sam Andrew knew that Janis's powerful and gritty vocals perfectly fit the sound he called the "progressive regressive hurricane blues."

Janis threw herself headlong into the "hurricane," giving the band—and the music—everything she had. Of those first live performances, she said, "The music was boom, boom, boom and the people were all dancing, and the lights, and I was standing up there singing into the microphone and getting it on, and whew! I dug it. So I said, 'I think I'll stay, boys.'"

In order to be heard over the instruments, she pushed her voice to the edge. Rough and raucous, the results were so loud and sometimes so distorted that one night, while the band rehearsed, the police showed up, saying they'd gotten a report of a woman screaming. Not everyone thought Janis's raspy voice was a good addition to Big Brother, and at least a few friends told band members that they needed to "lose the chick" because she was so loud and brassy.

TICKET OUTLETS - SAN FRANCISCO: MNASIDIKA (HAIGHT-ASHBURY), CITYLIGHTS BOOKS (N.BEACH), KELLEY GALLERIES (3681-A SACRAMENTO), THE TOWN SQUIRE (1318 POLK), BALLY LO SHOES (UNION SQ), HUT T-1 STATE COLLEGE. BEREKELY: MOES BOOKS, DISCOUNT RECORDS. SAUSALITO: TIDES BOOKSTORE REDWOOD CITY: REDWOOD HOUSE OF MUSIC (700 WINSLOW). SAN MATEO: TOWN & COUNTRY MUSIC CENTER (4TH & EL CAMINO), LA MER CAMERAS & MUSIC (HILLSDALE BLVD AT 19TH). MENLO PARK: KEPLER'S BOOKS & MAGAZINES (825 EL CAMINO). SAN JOSE: DISCORAMA (235 S. FIRST ST).

No.60-1

OPPOSITE: This Avalon Ballroom Dance concert poster depicts a God's eye, which is a symbol still used by Big Brother and the Holding Company. The poster advertises a concert that Big Brother played along with Blue Cheer and the Charlatans.

To work on unifying their sound and themselves—and to save on rent—the band, along with their respective spouses, lovers, children, and pets, packed up and moved to a hunting lodge in Lagunitas, north of San Francisco in Marin County. In this rural retreat, with few neighbors to be bothered by the noise (except for the Grateful Dead, who had shacked up down the street and, anyway, were unlikely to mind), they lived together, got to know one another, and engaged in some serious rehearsing and songwriting.

It was a happy time. Janis began a relationship with Joe McDonald of the band Country Joe and the Fish. It lasted only a few months, but that was long enough for McDonald to see Janis's softer side. To him, she was disarmingly sweet. He recalled dancing and flirting with her the first night they were together in Lagunitas, and later going home to her apartment in the Haight. "It was totally furnished with Victorian fru fru," he recalled. "There was always herbal tea on the stove and it was very warm and cozy." He reminisced about nights when the two of them would stay up late and call a local radio station to ask the DJ to play their songs. "[A]nd we were so happy about that," he said.

But when Janis began to do drugs again, McDonald saw her darker side. He said that some of her band mates, their partners, and even groupies or hangers-on would push Janis to shoot up, get loud, "scream and yell and screech . . ." They loved to see her get crazy. It was part of her image: the wild woman, the blues mama. It was as if people were disappointed if she wasn't outrageous and going to extremes. It became nearly impossible for Janis to avoid alcohol and drugs.

Over time, the band gelled both musically and personally. Its sound—a blend of folk and blues—evolved in the process and was beginning to grab attention beyond San Francisco.

DANCE CONCERT
AVALON BALLROOM
SAN FRANCISCO
PRESENTS
TICKET OUTLETS - SAN FRANCISCO: MNASIDKA (HAIGHT-ASHBURY), CITYLIGHTS BOOKS (NO.BEACH), KELLY GALLERIES (3681-A SACRAMENTO), THE TOWN SQUIRE (1318 POLK ST), BALLY LO SHOES (UNION SQ), HUT T-1 STATE COLLEGE. BERKELY: MOES BOOKS, DISCOUNT RECORDS. SAUSALITO: TIDES BOOKSTORE. REDWOOD CITY: REDWOOD HOUSE OF MUSIC (700 WINSTON). SAN MATEO: TOWN & COUNTRY MUSIC CENTER (4TH & EL CAMINO), LA MER CAMERAS & MUSIC (HILLSDALE BLVD AT 19TH). MENLO PARK: KEPLER'S BOOKS & MAGAZINES (825 EL CAMINO). SAN JOSE: DISCORAMA (235 S. FIRST ST)
No.55-1
1967 © FAMILY DOG PRODUCTIONS 639 GOUGH ST., San Francisco, Calif. 94102

SUTTER AT VAN NESS
SAN FRANCISCO
BIG BROTHER & THE HOLDING CO.
THURSDAY AND FRIDAY ONLY
MOUNT RUSHMORE
THURSDAY THROUGH SUNDAY
CANNED HEAT
SATURDAY AND SUNDAY ONLY
MOTHER EARTH
SATURDAY AND SUNDAY ONLY
LIGHTS · THE NORTH AMERICAN IBIS ALCHEMICAL COMPANY
1967 · DENNIS NOLAN
TICKET OUTLETS - SAN FRANCISCO: MNASIDKA (HAIGHT-ASHBURY), MIDDLE EARTH (852 STANYAN), CITYLIGHTS BOOKS (NORTH BEACH), THE TOWN SQUIRE (1318 POLK). BERKELEY: DISCOUNT RECORDS, ELECTRIC TIBET. SAUSALITO: TIDES BOOKSTORE. REDWOOD CITY: REDWOOD HOUSE OF MUSIC (700 WINSLOW). SAN MATEO: TOWN & COUNTRY MUSIC CENTER (4TH & EL CAMINO), LA MER CAMERAS & MUSIC (HILLSDALE AT 19TH). MENLO PARK: KEPLERS BOOKS AND MAGAZINES (825 EL CAMINO). SAN JOSE: DISCORAMA (235 S. FIRST ST).

Janis blended her own gravelly blues with the sweet soul sound of a favorite singer, Otis Redding, mimicking the frank, emotional way he crooned ballads.

In August 1966, Big Brother began recording its first album with the music company Mainstream Records. Mainstream wanted a radio-friendly sound, which wasn't compatible with the more experiential, free-flowing instrumentation of psychedelic rock. The band was disappointed with the tinny cuts Mainstream produced. They didn't do justice to the meandering guitar riffs, surprising melodies, and pounding beats the band was known to provide live audiences.

Onstage they were a powerhouse of sound, playing to packed theaters almost every night, interacting with the audience and each other, but their recordings reflected none of the thrills and spontaneity of their live performances. As Janis explained to one interviewer, "I do believe in some very amorphous things that happen when you're on stage . . . like something moves in the air."

When the songs were released ahead of the album as 45 rpm singles, no one was surprised that they failed to get radio attention. This just confirmed the band's belief that live rock shows were the real way to experience their music.

True to their belief, in the upcoming year, it would be their performances, and not their recordings, which would propel Big Brother forward, into the realm of rock superstardom. While Janis was already a spectacular, larger-than-life presence, she was still, in late 1966, considered just one of the band, often standing to the side while her band mates played long, wandering acid riffs. That was all about to change.

OPPOSITE: Chet Helms's concert promotion company, Family Dog, created this poster using illustrations of Big Brother and the Holding Company band members. Janis is in the upper left corner.

ABOVE: This Big Brother album cover demonstrates Janis's rise to fame after the Monterey International Pop Festival. The album, released after the festival, features Janis with the other members of the band.

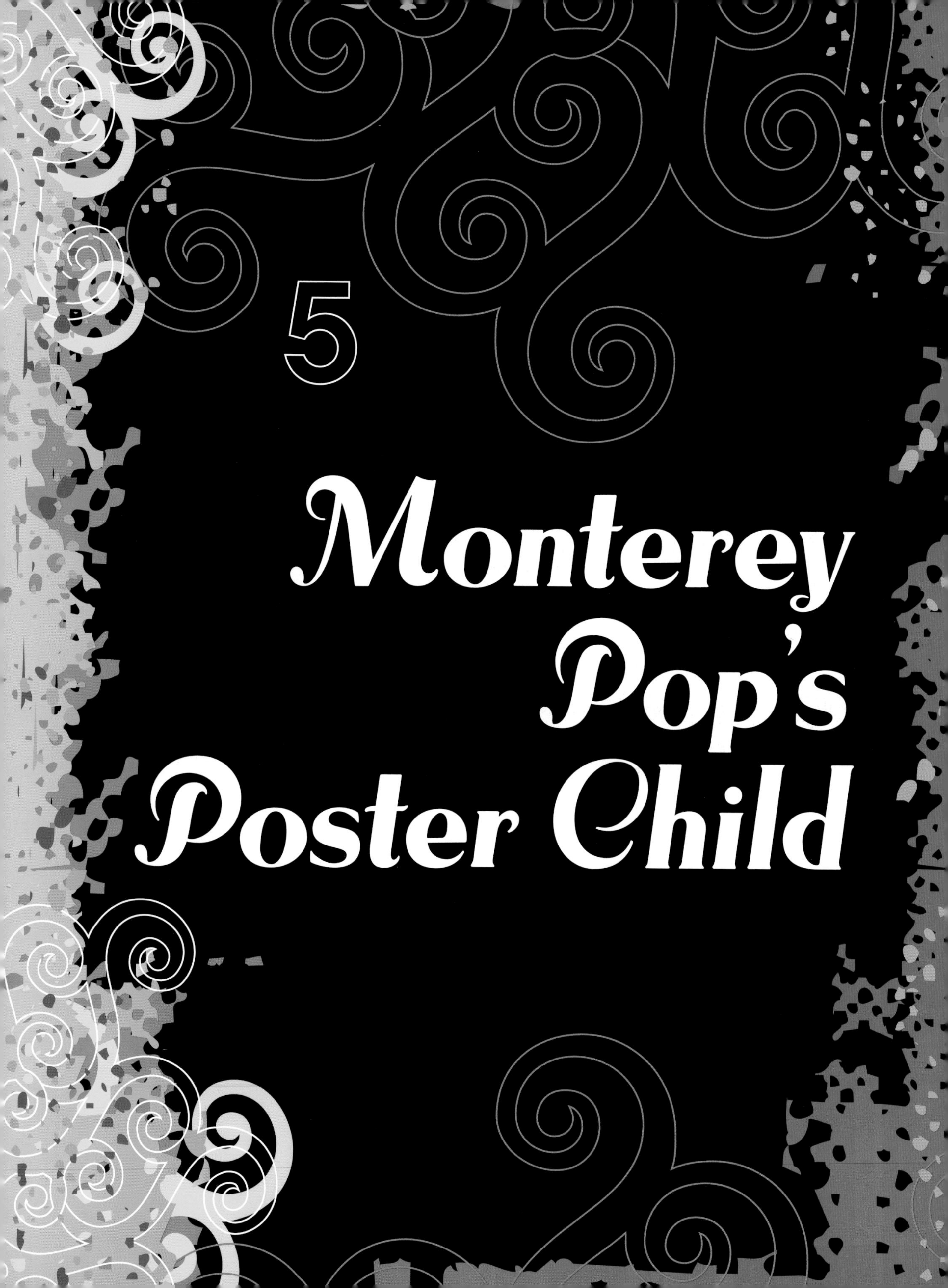
5
Monterey Pop's Poster Child

Folk singer Joan Baez sits at the corner of Haight and Ashbury in San Francisco, serenading hippies and tourists, September 1967.

By 1967 thousands of young people were pouring into San Francisco, attracted by the message of the flower children of the Haight. With the United States engaged in what would be a long and deadly war in Vietnam, the hippies' message of peace, love, and tolerance for all people was alluring, particularly to those who thought the war was wrong or feared being drafted.

The highlight of the year was the Summer of Love. It officially began in June with the Monterey International Pop Festival, where Big Brother and the Holding Company, along with dozens of other acts, were scheduled to appear.

This festival, the biggest event of the season and the first outdoor musical event of this magnitude, was set for the weekend of June 16. Organized by pop music tycoon Lou Adler and John Phillips of the band the Mamas and the Papas, it drew more than fifty thousand people, eager to experience what Phillips declared "the summer of free love and rock and roll." The musicians played for free; profits from a planned film of the event were to be donated to charities, such as the San Francisco Diggers, an organization that, among other things, opened and operated stores that simply gave away their stock to anyone who needed it.

By the time Big Brother and the Holding Company took the stage on Saturday afternoon, the sun had burned off the morning mist and had begun to beat down on the crowd. Fans, dressed in feathers and beads, fringed suede, and jeans or miniskirts, with psychedelic flowers and peace signs painted on their cheeks, were gathered peacefully under brightly colored banners that billowed in the wind.

Dave Getz jumped to the stage and settled in behind his drums. Sam Andrew, Peter Albin, and James Gurley joined him, strapping guitars across their chests. Once the band was in place, a lone electric guitar squealed the opening chords of "Ball and Chain," a rock adaptation of the old blues song, as a young woman in blue jeans and a peasant shirt, her face framed by long frizzy hair, skipped on to the stage. Janis, known to few outside of the San Francisco scene, looked like any other hippie girl. But then she began to sing.

Her voice purred and rose in a wail that sent shivers through the crowd. She swung her hair and stomped her foot, moaning, "Oh, oh, o-oo-wowo-waha . . . honey, tell me why, why does everything go wrong?" And then her voice escalated in a keening scream, "Oh people, it ain't fair

Janis backstage at the Winterland Ballroom on New Year's Eve, 1967.

what you do." She held the microphone close to her lips, like she was kissing it, as she sent her wild-woman sounds into the world. It was as if she was calling everyone to hear her sad story, to feel her agony, her longing and pain. With eyes closed, she wrung the blues out of "Down on Me." She cried into the mic, "Everybody in this whole damn world is down on me. . . ." When the song ended, all eyes were locked on her.

In the front row of the audience, Cass Elliot of the Mamas and the Papas sat stunned, her lips forming just one word over and over and over again: "Wow!" This summed it up—the crowd had never seen or heard anyone like Janis.

ROLLING STONE

ACME

FEBRUARY 24, 1968
VOL. I, No. 6

OUR PRICE:
TWENTY-FIVE CENTS

MONTEREY FESTIVAL ON AGAIN; ROME SHOW OFF

It Happened In 1967

For the ROLLING STONE AWARDS and first annual "Look Back In Anger" review of the year past, see Page 11. Janis Joplin, a winner, is shown above; a scene from the Gathering of the Tribes, another winner, below.
PHOTOGRAPHS BY BARON WOLMAN

Adler Given First Shot at Fairgrounds

BY MICHAEL LYDON

The Monterey International Pop Festival is going to happen again—maybe, and — maybe again—the Festival will soon have straightened out the financial mess left after Monterey 1967.

Festival producer Lou Adler has spoken with George Wise, manager of the Monterey County Fairgrounds where the first festival was held, and asked that the grounds be tentatively reserved for June 21, 22, 23. Adler, who ran last year's Festival with John Phillips, has been unreachable, but friends say he is enthusiastic about the prospect of another one.

But so far no staff has been hired, and since first speaking with Wise early in January, Adler has done nothing to confirm the dates. "All he has to do is call," says Wise. "I liked working with Adler's group last year, and I am giving them first priority. But they will have to speak soon."

Adler has to decide because Charles Royal, publisher of Roy-

—Continued on Page 4

Rome 'Festival' Turns Out to Be Small Time Job

Out of the murk of small time promoters came the name of the "First International European Pop Festival," and back into the murk it has slipped, perhaps never to be heard from again. Originally planned for February, it has been postponed to May and may never come off at all.

The Festival, which had a letterhead, a few representatives in various capitals and, so says rumor, a pair of rich Americans and an Italian prince behind it, was scheduled for February 19 through 25 at Rome's Palazzo dello Sport. Over a dozen English groups were claimed to have signed, Country Joe and the Fish did sign a contract, and other American (mostly San Francisco) groups agreed to appear pending signing of contracts.

But late in January groups which had agreed got terse telegrams signed "First International European Pop Festival." The telegrams read: "Festival set back May-June; Sicilian disaster; delayed American acceptances; requests for delay for more widespread international representation; publicity; and backer's orders. Festival will happen. New negotiations within 30 days."

—Continued on Page 22

BOB DYLAN COMES OUT AT WOODY MEMORIAL

BY SUE C. CLARK

NEW YORK

Bob Dylan finally emerged from 18 months of self-imposed seclusion at the Woody Guthrie Memorial Concert in Carnegie Hall on January 20. His appearance had been announced and the two performances were sold out weeks in advance. Scalpers were reportedly getting $25.00 per ticket, and at the concert itself people were standing on the sidewalk and in the lobby begging, "Extra tickets? Any tickets for sale?"

In addition to Dylan, the memorial concert also featured Pete Seeger, Judy Collins, Woody's son Arlo Guthrie, Tom Paxton, Jack Elliot, Odetta and Richie Havens, all performing songs written by Guthrie. Before and after each song, Robert Ryan, the program's narrator, and Will Geer did readings from Guthrie's work, accompanied by slides and still photographs of his art.

The performers sat in a row across the stage, most of them resplendently dressed. Odetta wore an orange and gold striped floor-length caftan, Judy Collins sported a red rose at the neck of her long-sleeved white blouse, while Richie Havens had on a purple silk Indian shirt beneath a black Nehru suit with a long jacket. But Bob Dylan, in a gunmetal grey silk mohair suit, blue shirt with green jewels for cuff links and black suede boots as well as his new beard and moustache, was the center of attention.

Most of the artists accompa-

—Continued on Page 2

OPPOSITE: Janis became the face of the Monterey International Pop Festival; *Rolling Stone* magazine put Janis on the front page of an issue covering the big rock events of 1967.

LEFT: *Live at Winterland '68* was produced with Janis's name prominently displayed on the album cover as the band's star.

It was a turning point. With this performance, Janis became a star. A documentary filmmaker, D. A. Pennebaker, who shot much of the event, caught just a short clip of the band's second Sunday-evening performance, but he used Janis's "Down on Me" as the soundtrack for the film credits. Her voice embodied the spirit of the festival and the social and political ideals of this new generation.

For Janis, Monterey was a harbinger of fame and fortune. A *Rolling Stone* critic reported that she "brought the house down belting out the blues with her magnificent voice" and christened her a rock star, claiming that she had joined rock-and-roll royalty and the ranks of the wild guys—Bob Dylan, Jim Morrison, and Jimi Hendrix, who ended his own star-making Monterey performance by setting his guitar on fire with lighter fluid and smashing it to bits. Janis, with her powerful, unrestrained sound and sexually charged performances, so different from the polished looks and singing of previous female stars, was poised to change the history of women in rock and roll forever.

Big Brother and the Holding Company considered this photo as a possible album cover for their second album.

When the festival was over, Janis partied with Jimi Hendrix and members of the Grateful Dead and Jefferson Airplane. Everyone was high. People were smoking grass and dropping acid. Hendrix more than anyone. Sam Andrew described the little white pills in Hendrix's hands that night as looking like candy: "I thought it was Tic Tacs, he was taking so many of them."

The drugs surrounding Janis that night were another harbinger, but a darker one. In the years to follow, she would become legendary for her partying and for her unquenchable thirst for booze and heroin. In fact, it wouldn't be long before Janis's demons—her wild addictions—would threaten to overwhelm her career.

In August 1967, Janis's family visited San Francisco to check on her. Janis, who coveted her parents' approval even if she wasn't living how they'd hoped she would, was excited to show them her life and her new "pad," which she'd decorated like a harem room, with madras and lots of pillows, feathers, lace, and posters of her friends and idols. As her sister, Laura, described, "[Janis] was skipping around, showing us around Golden Gate Park.

She took us to her apartment and there was an entire wall of Janis nude." (The nudes were taken by photographer Bob Siedeman, who also photographed Janis and the band for a series of posters created to promote their performances at the Avalon.)

Later, she took her family to the Avalon, where they heard her perform. Afterward, outside the club, she asked, "Isn't it wonderful? . . . Oh, can't you see?" Laura described the moment: "Caught between two worlds, [Janis] stood, perplexed, believing that we should like it. I think Janis realized then that we didn't, and couldn't, and probably weren't going to see." Though Janis's parents would never understand their daughter's music or lifestyle, their visit proved to her that they took pride in her accomplishments and gave her the security of knowing that she could always go home again.

Despite their fundamental differences, Dorothy Joplin regularly wrote or talked to her oldest daughter on the phone about "ideas about things and songs," and about her music career. Janis's letters in response, often written when the band was on the road, showed a loving interest in her family. She "talked" to each of them in turn, encouraging her younger brother, Michael, to listen to a new song and offering Laura fashion advice. As Laura described, these letters, many of which are very long, are "rich in detail of what she was feeling, experiencing." In them, she drew a picture of her world, conveying the scene through details: "A fashion note—thought y'all would like to know what everyone looks like out here. The girls are, of course, young & beautiful looking w/long straight hair. . . . But the boys are the real peacocks. All have their hair at least Beatle length." She seemed to particularly enjoy describing clothes she had bought or had had a friend sew for her.

As the band's fame grew, their finances improved, and Janis embraced the outrageous opportunities success afforded her. She dressed in feathers, fur, silk, and beads. She traded in the beat-up Morris Minor on which poster-artist Stanley Mouse had painted a God's eye (to advertise Big Brother) for a Porsche painted with psychedelic butterflies and flowers. The car became a favorite sight in San Francisco and fans would leave notes under the wiper blades for Janis wherever they found it parked.

Janis craved the attention. She posed for posters and pictures. While touring with the band, she hung out in the streets and in local parks with fans and friends, even partying with members of the Hells Angels, a motorcycle gang that sometimes provided security for concerts. While the music was her life force, adulation fed her spirit.

OPPOSITE: Janis sits on a motorcycle in Columbus, Ohio.

BELOW: This Gulf Coast Museum exhibit shows Janis's second painted car, a Porsche. The paintings on the walls in the background are by Janis.

For Janis, Monterey was her golden moment. Long after her reputation as the queen of rock and roll had solidified, and the music had gained wide commercial appeal, she looked back on that summer weekend in 1967 and reminisced, "The best time of all was Monterey. It was one of the highest points of my life. Those were real flower children. They really were beautiful and gentle and open, man. Ain't nothing like that going to happen again. But for awhile, there were kids who believed they could make it all better and it didn't make a bit of difference."

Acclaim brought Janis and Big Brother a new manager, Albert Grossman, a New York heavyweight who was also Bob Dylan's manager. Grossman quickly snagged the group a recording contract with Columbia Records, one of the country's most powerful music companies, and the band prepared to record what was expected to be a blockbuster album.

But acclaim also caused power struggles within the band. As Getz remembers, "We felt we had a fabulous weapon with Janis. [But] Peter was the leader of the band." Though Peter Albin had always been the band's spokesman, band members accused Janis of vying for the role. Getz recalled watching the documentary of the Monterey Festival and realizing, "There was something wrong, that it was just Janis, the band wasn't in the movie."

Myra Friedman, the band's new publicist at Albert Grossman's agency, lined up interviews with the New York media, part of Grossman's campaign to build interest in the band before the release of their Columbia album. Although Friedman tried to get reporters to meet with the whole group, they seemed interested only in the fascinatingly seductive chick singer with the amazing voice.

OPPOSITE: This photo of Big Brother and the Holding Company in front of an American flag may have been considered for an album cover. It was taken in Lagunitas, California, where the band rented a house. Clockwise from bottom are Janis, Sam Andrew, Peter Albin, James Gurley, and David Getz.

In the thick of this success, Janis, the triumphant rock star, returned to Port Arthur for Christmas, bearing gifts from her travels and chatting excitedly about her career. Her cheer, however, masked an unhappy secret: She was pregnant and had made the decision to slip into Mexico for an abortion when the band was scheduled to play in Southern California in January. The baby's father was no longer in the picture, and Janis didn't believe that she could have a child and sustain her career.

Abortion wasn't legal in the United States in 1967, and health care in Mexico wasn't as reliable as at home. Having an abortion was potentially life threatening. As Janis feared, the procedure didn't go well. Her healing was complicated by pain and hemorrhaging. Convinced that she'd never be able to have children afterward, she grieved her loss. She had never let go of the idea of marriage and a family, of the path her high school classmates had taken, even as her life spun in a very different direction.

Though Janis's personal life was becoming more and more troubled, her public life continued to blossom. That same month, *Rolling Stone* called her "possibly the best female voice of her generation." A few weeks later, the *Village Voice* declared, "The plumage and the punch in the last few years' rock has remained in the province of men. . . . Now, with Janis all that is over."

Despite the praise, Janis worried about the quality of the band's sound and their appearance. "We're just a sloppy group of street freaks," she confided to Friedman. And despite fame, she still fretted about her looks. Between performances, she studied herself in the mirror and asked Friedman, "Do I look old?" Anxiety dragged her down, sometimes to a dark emotional place. "I certainly think she was prone to depression," said Friedman. "She was morbidly depressed at times." But her humor and wild partying hid the pain from most. "[She was] often revved up," recalled Friedman, "but there were times if you watched her . . . you could see."

Albert Grossman took advantage of the band's strong reviews and scheduled a U.S. tour that would begin in February 1968. Beforehand, however, he made a telling change to the band's billing: From now on, they would be known as "Big Brother and the Holding Company, featuring Janis Joplin." Janis was the big draw now. In a letter to her family, dated January 31, 1968, Janis wrote, "Twenty-five. 25. XXV. A quarter of a century! Oh, it's all too incredible. . . . I never thought I'd even survive this long."

Janis sings at the Fillmore East in New York City, 1969.

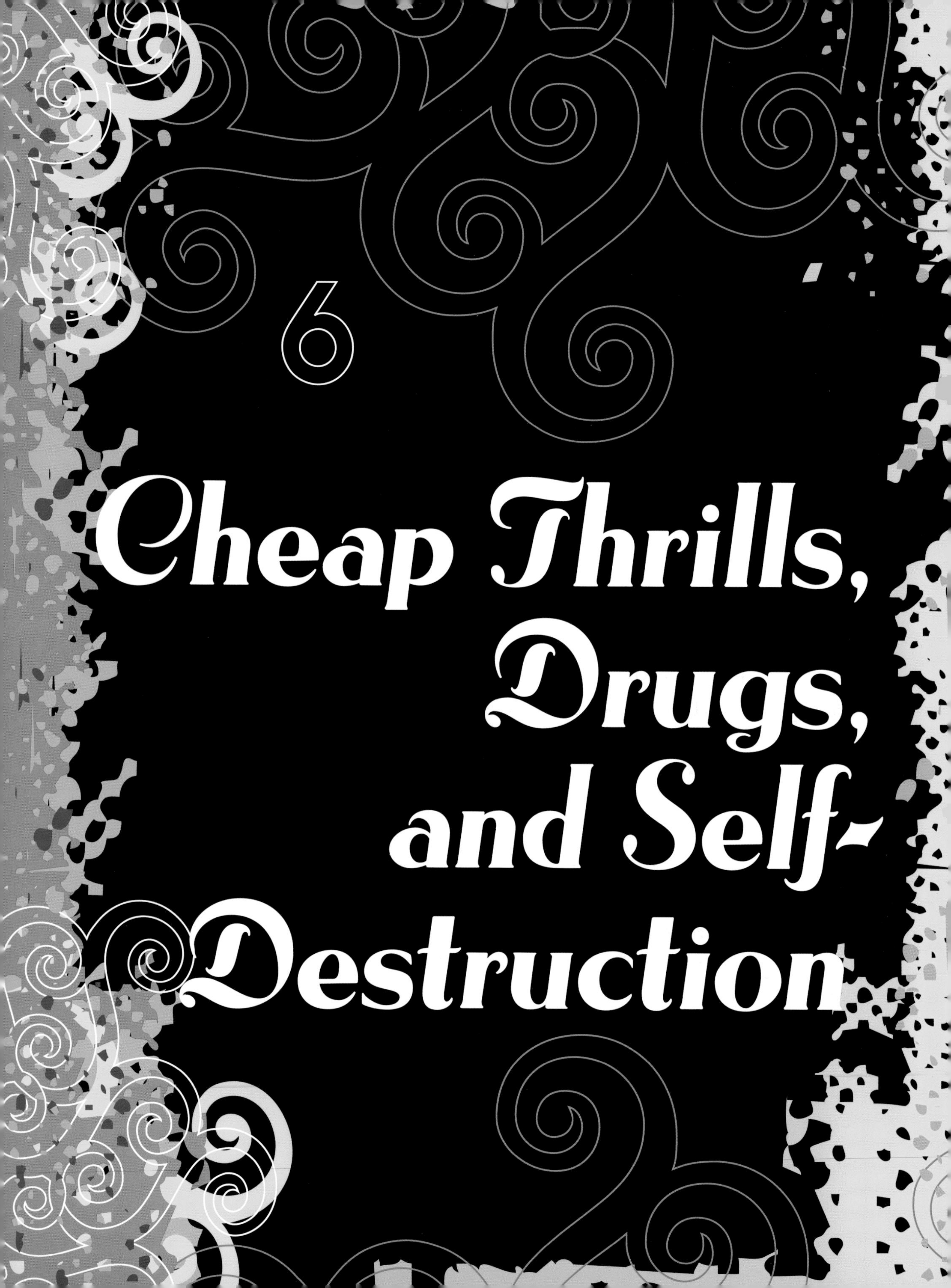

6

Cheap Thrills, Drugs, and Self-Destruction

By 1968 the recording industry had fully embraced psychedelic rock. Jimi Hendrix watched his single "Purple Haze" remain on *Billboard's* top 10 list for half the year. And when San Francisco band Jefferson Airplane put out its fourth album, it sold more than one million copies and was promptly certified gold.

But the improvisational sound of psychedelic rock remained tricky to capture on vinyl. The Grateful Dead began experimenting in the recording studio with free-form music, hoping to replicate the trippy, flowing sound of its live performances. Big Brother was recording as well, trusting that Columbia Records would do a better job than Mainstream of capturing the essence of a live show. Columbia expected great sales for this new album, tentatively titled *Dope, Sex and Cheap Thrills*. For the band, pressure grew from trying to wedge their experimental sound into a tight commercial format.

Janis knew what she liked and disliked musically, and she spent many hours working to shape the album to her tastes and ideas. Her strong work ethic drove her to attain a higher sound quality, especially in her vocals. At times, nothing seemed to be coming together, and tension within the band grew thick. One night, the group was in the studio for hours, recording take after take; Janis's vocals were dead-on every try, but the band kept making mistakes. Finally Janis stormed out, screaming, "I ain't going to sing with those motherfuckers!" She was beginning to wonder if it was time to leave Big Brother.

Despite her doubts, there were beautiful moments in the studio. When the band got it right, as they did with the opening licks of "Summertime," it was real-life magic: ethereal, crystal-clear guitar flowing in and around Janis's raspy voice as she pleaded, "Hush little baby . . . nonononono don't you cryyyyyyy."

But outside the studio, the world had turned ugly. On April 4, 1968, Martin Luther King Jr., the prominent peace activist and civil rights leader, who had done much to advance the cause of blacks and people of color, was assassinated in Memphis.

Big Brother and the Holding Company took the stage, along with many other musicians, in a tribute held at the Generation Club in New York City. As Sam Andrew recalled, "Emotions were running very high as a lot of cities all around the country were in flames. . . . B. B. King sat backstage and talked about the tragedy in a very emotional, beautiful, calm manner. He made us feel the dignity and the poignancy of the moment. It was like being in church to hear him talk of the need for understanding and love between the brothers and the sisters, oh, yes, all over this world."

The *Cheap Thrills* album cover was designed by counterculture cartoonist R. Crumb. The band originally planned to call the album *Dope, Sex and Cheap Thrills*.

The ideals of the Summer of Love were badly shaken. As the Vietnam War raged on and the civil rights movement reached a fevered pitch, the band, now called Janis Joplin and Big Brother and the Holding Company, kept so busy in April that life felt like an out-of-control carnival ride. They played ABC-TV's *Hollywood Palace*, performed and created a live recording at Winterland in San Francisco, continued studio sessions at Columbia's Hollywood studio, and performed at San Fernando Valley College. They returned to New York in June to complete recording the album that was now simply called *Cheap Thrills*. "Even then," said their road manager, John Byrne Cooke, "the community of those whose music was turning on the younger generations was fairly small. We traveled around the country at a time when . . . rock wasn't big business yet, but the major record companies were lurking around the edges, signing one act and then another. Things changed quite fast after that. Not for the better." Cooke disliked the materialism and greed of

the recording industry, and the way talent was considered a commodity to be harnessed for profit. It was not in keeping with the spirit of the hippie movement, in which music was something to be shared and enjoyed freely. Now the sound that had emerged in carefree days and nights in Haight-Ashbury had become big, serious business.

Friction among band members continued to build as they started to get bad press after live performances, especially in New York. Critics fed Janis's ego when they encouraged her to get stronger musicians to support her sound. *Rolling Stone* called the band "messy and a general musical disgrace." And Michael Bloomfield, himself a skilled guitarist, slammed the band in *Rolling Stone* while praising Janis, writing, "Big Brother is just a wretched, lame group of cats who she carries for no reason at all."

By the summer of 1968, when Big Brother was invited to perform at the Newport Folk Festival, they were so unhappy that a couple of band members were regularly injecting heroin to numb themselves. Janis was seriously considering going off on her own, but the thought tore at her. She knew that she could reach higher levels of musical excellence if her voice was supported by trained musicians—the guys in Big Brother, like many musicians from the psychedelic tradition, were self-taught and still learning—but she had lived closely with the band, day after day, through months of touring and recording. They were like family.

In the face of so much pressure, Janis was almost always loaded, both onstage and off. By now drugs and booze were established parts of both her celebrity image and her personal life. She usually arrived onstage for a show with a bottle of Southern Comfort in hand, eventually getting the company to reward her for the free publicity. As she told the *New York Times Magazine*, "I had the chick in my manager's office photostat every goddamn clipping that ever had me mentioning Southern Comfort, and I sent them to the company, and they sent me a whole lotta money. How could anybody in their right mind want me for their image? Oh man, that was the best hustle I ever pulled—can you imagine getting paid for passing out for two years?" The company even bought her a lynx coat as thanks.

But this humor about drinking and getting high masked what was becoming a serious problem. In interviews, Janis alluded to drug use, often romanticizing its role in her music. One friend recalled, "[Janis] said it was the blues-singer mystique, like Billie Holiday, to get real messed up." And following Newport, Janis herself told a *Time* reporter, "When I go onstage to sing, it's like the 'rush' that people experience when they take heavy dope. I talk to the audience, look in their eyes. I need them and they need me. Sex is the closest I can come to explaining it, but it's more than sex." She added, "I get stoned from happiness. I want to do it until it isn't there any more."

Clearly, part of the problem was that her fans reveled in her outrageous behavior. Not only did they expect her to be out of control, they encouraged and rewarded it; the crazier and freer she got, the more popular she became. Then, too, there was the issue of bridging the gap between performing and real life, and of making the everyday as thrilling and compelling as performing. As James Gurley explained, "Performing with Janis was an adrenaline-raising thing. I would never be able to go to sleep past dawn. . . . And so, there was always wanting something that would cool you out." Though alcohol was clearly Janis's preferred drug, she was dabbling in heroin more and more. Mixed, the two could be a deadly combination. As Laura attested, "Janis was no longer controlling her life. It was controlling her."

By June of that year, the studio had produced more than two hundred reels of audiotape for *Cheap Thrills.* Pre-sale orders were off the charts, and the album was certified gold before it was even available. In August, it was released to critical acclaim. Big Brother was now a national success, but according to Getz, "It was too late. . . . By the end of the summer of 1968, when [Janis] came into the room at the Chelsea [Hotel] and said she was leaving, it was no surprise." Janis later told a reporter, "I love those guys more than anybody else in the whole world, they know that. But if I had any serious idea of myself as a musician, I had to leave."

The band played together a few more times, returning to San Francisco to perform their final gig at the Palace of Fine Arts Festival from August 30 through September 1. After that, manager Albert Grossman announced an "amicable split" between Janis and Big Brother. Janis was free to hire a new band and move on.

OPPOSITE: A photo of an exhausted Janis, who appears to have spent all her passion performing at the Newport Folk Festival.

7

Kozmic Blues

When Janis formed Kozmic Blues, Sam Andrew came along to play guitar.

Janis admitted that she had a bad case of the blues during the year she worked with her new band, the Kozmic Blues. With only three weeks to prepare for their debut, the group didn't have time to get to know each other, let alone establish their sound. The problem wasn't just that the heady mix of horns and percussion overwhelmed even Janis's powerful voice; the band members failed to work well as a group, and Janis was unsure of herself as their leader. Although Big Brother band mate Sam Andrew was part of the Kozmic Blues, Janis missed the camaraderie they'd had with Big Brother.

The Kozmic Blues premiered on December 21, 1968, at the Stax-Volt Convention Center in Memphis. The following night the band was billed second on a list of professional soul acts at the Mid-South Coliseum, also in Memphis. They received a cool reception. Although critics praised Janis's voice, their reviews of the band were lukewarm at best.

February's Fillmore East show didn't offer much hope that the Kozmic Blues would crystallize. Again, reviews were mixed. In March the group made an appearance on *The Ed Sullivan Show*, the popular TV program that had showcased famous rock acts such as Elvis Presley and the Beatles. Their performance left listeners less than thrilled.

According to Myra Friedman, although band members were listless and detached, "Janis's performance of 'Maybe' was out and out sublime. A number of musicians were there, to begin with, only as a business venture. Nevertheless, Janis's state of mind, her intensity coupled with insecurity, her drive accompanied by her ability to demand center stage and her unquenchable appetite to be high did little to lift their spirits and much to increase their attitudes that backing up Janis was, after all, nothing more than a job." Reviews such as Ralph J. Gleason's in the *San Francisco Chronicle*, suggesting that Janis "go back to Big Brother if they'll have her," stung.

April and May 1969 brought a more successful European tour, with shows in Amsterdam, Paris, and England. Each time she performed, Janis dove into the song, putting all of her emotion into the music. Her long hair flying around her face and sticking to her sweat-soaked cheeks, she stomped her feet, sometimes rising up on her toes to capture a high note, swinging and swaying to the beat of the music. She would scream, "I'm gonna try . . . ," picking up the tempo, "try, try, try . . . ," and reaching a crescendo of sound, "so I won't lose, lose, lose you . . ." Onstage, she never stopped moving—or trying. The European audiences were hooked. The *New Musical Express* called Janis's British debut a triumph that "left most of the audience on their feet yelling for more."

Upon their return to the United States on July 18, 1969, Janis and the Kozmic Blues performed on *The Dick Cavett Show*, the most popular television talk show. In his introduction, Cavett quoted a *Newsweek* cover story that had reported that Janis "blew the rock world wide open, singing with a tortured passion that has become her trademark." The article proclaimed Janis to be "the first female superstar of rock music."

OPPOSITE: According to Janis's publicist and friend, Myra Friedman, this Kozmic Blues album cover was intended to depict the cosmic nature and mind-expanding experience of the blues.

OVERLEAF: This sequence gives a sense of the energy and feeling she brought to her performances.

In the interview, Janis, shyly smiling, sat beside Cavett. Appearing unsure of herself, she rubbed her hands together while her eyes darted back and forth nervously from Cavett to the audience. When Cavett asked how the European tour had gone, Janis commented that European audiences, which she had managed to coax to their feet to dance in the aisles, were too cerebral. "They don't get down," she said, releasing her familiar cackle of a laugh. Relaxing a bit, she pulled out a cigarette.

Cavett held up a lighter and asked, "Can I light your fire?" When the lighter failed to ignite, Janis giggled and replied, "Apparently not." Her flirtatious manner obviously delighted her host; Janis relaxed, and the two bantered easily. Comparing Janis to Cass Elliot of the Mamas and the Papas and to Grace Slick of Jefferson Airplane, Cavett asked why so few women become rock superstars. Although she chuckled, Janis's response demonstrated serious consideration of her career. "I don't know; it's not feminine maybe—to get down, get on the bottom side of music," she said. She explained that most female musicians seemed to float over the music when they sang rather than to get down and mine the deep emotion of it.

Janis's emotional, no-limits style was fundamental to her image. She loved the attention she'd get for living "fast" and for saying and doing shocking things. In a *New York Times Magazine* article, she confessed, "Yeah, I know I might be going too fast. That's what a doctor said. He looked at me and said my liver is a little big, swollen, y'know. Got all melodramatic—'what's a good, talented girl doing with yourself' and all that blah blah. I don't go to him anymore. Man, I'd rather have ten years of superhypermost than live to be seventy sitting in some goddamn chair watching TV."

Friedman believes that Janis called attention to herself because it fed her need to be loved. Sometimes Janis was so demanding of attention that her good friends got fed up. Friedman described times when the two would go out for a drink and Janis would wrap herself in her lynx coat and, playing up her celebrity, cockily ask the doorman or taxi driver if he knew who she was; then, she'd tell whoever would listen that she was a rock star. In those moments, Friedman said, "I told her to cut it out."

On most of those nights out, Janis and Friedman had fun. They shared laughs and serious talks about life, love, and the arts. Friedman recalled Janis being outlandish one minute, "absolutely hysterical" the next, then turning the discussion to world news or a book she had just read. "She was brilliant, and very well read."

Exceedingly ambitious, Janis was also a savvy, hard-working businesswoman who made the most of her fame. She performed more than a hundred live concerts in three years and had the sense and forethought to create a corporation, Fantality, to merchandise fan memorabilia. She also developed a publishing company, Strong Arm Music. Though she was loose and out of control in many

OPPOSITE: Janis joins Tina Turner for a song in New York's Madison Square Garden during the Rolling Stones' Thanksgiving concert in 1969.

OPPOSITE: This photo from the Newport Folk Festival shows Janis's style beginning to evolve away from the earlier Beat influence to reflect her role as a star. Janis, who performed at the festival in 1968 and 1969, often played percussion instruments such as the maracas while onstage.

aspects of her life, she almost never lost sight of her fundamental desire to make music.

Janis was among the biggest rock acts of the era, which was about to host its biggest musical extravaganza ever: the Woodstock Music & Art Fair. The dates of the event, August 15 to 17, 1969, live in many people's minds as the greatest in music history, at least in part for the temporary antidote it offered to concerns about the brutal Vietnam War and ugly racial tensions.

Woodstock was and has remained a landmark of the 1960s, despite the notorious rain and mud, bad acid, and inadequate planning. For three days, a slew of celebrated rock stars, including Janis Joplin, Jimi Hendrix, and Joe Cocker, played the stage in Bethel, New York, to a crowd of almost half a million people. After the festival, Janis observed, "We don't need a leader. We have each other. All we need is to keep our heads straight and in ten years this country may be a decent place to live."

The Kozmic Blues band toured heavily throughout the rest of the year. Janis pushed herself harder and harder, punishing her voice each night with too much alcohol and too little time to rest between performances. After concerts, she sounded raspy and strained, and people began to comment that she was ruining her voice.

Janis's concerts were wild affairs, played to packed houses. Her need for adulation and human connection drove her mesmerizing performances. She cried to the crowd and urged them to get up and dance with her. Their frenzy made her high, fed something in her, filled some hole. As she poured out her emotions to the crowd, they, in turn, flooded her with adoration.

Some communities became concerned about the safety of her shows, about the possibility of drug overdoses or of fans being hurt when, overcome with feeling, they rushed

OPPOSITE: The line on this *Rolling Stone* cover comparing Janis Joplin to the doomed star of a previous generation, Judy Garland, implied that people worried that Janis was self-destructing.

the stage. In November at a Tampa concert, police stormed the concert hall in an effort to control the audience, who were dancing in the aisles. "Listen," shouted Janis to the uniformed officers, "I know there won't be any trouble if you'll just leave!" When the officers tried to clear out the crowd instead, Janis let loose with a string of profanity that resulted in her arrest. Later, freed on bail, the singer was quoted in *Time* magazine as saying, "I don't mind getting arrested because I've turned a lot of kids on." The term "turn on" was slang that applied to introducing someone to sex, drugs, or rock and roll.

Offstage Janis surrounded herself with a growing entourage of groupies who invested little in their relationships with her. Usually stoned, they were there for the parties. Janis would slide in and out of one-night stands, never allowing herself to get too close to anyone. The temporary affection did little to ease her loneliness.

As the year drew to a close, Janis's drinking and heroin use were visibly affecting her performances. She knew she had to cut back or better yet quit, but where to draw the line and how? She had always equated letting go with following her heart, and breaking barriers with nonconformity. As her sister, Laura, explained, "She saw her choice as either abandoning the lifestyle that had brought her such acclaim and behaving like a schoolteacher in our hometown, or continuing the habits that she was seeking to quit. The way she framed the choice itself almost obligated her to deny recovery as a viable option. . . . Change was hard especially when the part of her that was demanding the change was corralled by such lethal barbed wire as heroin, alcohol, and superstar status."

By the end of 1969, a year marked by profound highs and devastating lows, Janis's world was veering out of control, and she knew that she needed a break.

A Report On
Janis Joplin:
The
Judy Garland
Of Rock?
ROLLING STONE
ACME
MARCH 15, 1969
NO. 29
UK: 3/6
35 CENTS
NEW BOB DYLAN
ALBUM FINISHED:
ALSO RECORDS
WITH JOHNNY CASH
Words About
Timothy Leary
Sports:
The Roller Derby
All the News
That Fits

8

To Love Somebody

Janis searched for a retreat, a place where she could escape insane work schedules and parties. She found it in a new home, surrounded by redwood trees, in the mountain community of Larkspur, California. She moved in December 1969. An article in *Time* magazine featured her new place in a report on the "psychedelic tie-dye look." The writer commented that many stars slept on tie-dyed sheets, noting, "Janis Joplin has a set in satin."

Janis's new home was cozy and warm, decorated with Victorian furniture, Oriental rugs, and lots of knickknacks. In a letter to her family, she described her new house enthusiastically, "It's turning into a palace—all fur & wood & stained glass & velvet couches & chaise lounges & even a chandelier hanging in the middle of an eye-full of redwoods. FANTASTIC!"

OPPOSITE: This August 6, 1970, cover of *Rolling Stone*, showing a smiling Janis, promises a glimpse of Janis with her new band, Full-Tilt Boogie.

By the end of 1969, the Kozmic Blues had played their last performance at Madison Square Garden. It was "a triumph" of sound that the band had not achieved previously. But Janis knew the group wasn't right for her, and they disbanded at the beginning of 1970.

Worn out, Janis made plans for her first real vacation in years, a trip with her friend Linda Gravenites to Rio de Janeiro, Brazil, to celebrate Carnival. The trip proved to be the source of renewal Janis needed. Not only did she go cold turkey—kicking heroin while she was away—but she fell for someone. Calling from Rio, she told a friend that she was "going off into the jungle with a big bear of a man." His name was David Niehaus, and she reported that she was in love with him.

But by March 28, she was back in Hollywood without Niehaus, cutting the song "One Night Stand" with Paul Butterfield. Though the two lovebirds had planned to return to California together, Niehaus had been detained in Brazil with a lapsed visa. Janis let her upset be an excuse to use drugs again. Niehaus arrived in Larkspur two days later to find Janis back on heroin, planning her upcoming tour.

Before long, Janis and Niehaus accepted that they wanted different things out of life and parted ways. As Janis explained it to her family in a letter home, "I met a really fine man in Rio but I had to get back to work so he's off finding the rest of the world—Africa or Morocco now I think, but he really did love me & was so good to me & he wants to come back & marry me! I thought I'd die without someone besides fans asking me. But he meant it & who knows—I may get tired of the music biz, but I'm really getting it on now!" The relationship, though happy and fulfilling in many ways to both of them, was never rekindled.

IND

ROLLING STONE
August 6, 1970
No. 64
UK: 3/-
50c
Janis Joplin
And Her New Full-Tilt Boogie Band
The View From The Mud:
A Special Section on Festivals
The Return of
Traffic
Wavy Gravy
And the Usual Trash.
Tony Lane

OPPOSITE: Kris Kristofferson, a scholar, movie star, and Janis's "thundering passion," also plays country music and is credited with giving Janis the song "Me and Bobby McGee."

Janis's affections soon shifted to Kris Kristofferson, a movie star, country singer, and Rhodes Scholar who Friedman called Janis's "thundering passion." They connected at a party that turned into a three-week drinking binge.

With the Kozmic Blues now out of the picture, some hoped that Janis would reunite with Big Brother—she performed with them a few times that spring. But she was in fact organizing a new band, one she now had the experience and confidence to lead. Only two members of Kozmic Blues, bassist Brad Campbell and lead guitarist John Till, who had replaced Sam Andrew, joined Full-Tilt Boogie. John Byrne Cooke remained as road manager. In May, Janis made her first appearance with the new band, debuting a stripped-down sound that allowed her to show off the full range of her voice.

Janis continued to see Kristofferson, who had his own reputation for hard drinking and partying, and he moved into her house for a time. At some point while they were together, he sang her a song he'd written called "Me and Bobby McGee," which she would include on the playlist for her upcoming album, *Pearl*. Although their relationship would soon end, perhaps because, as Kristofferson admitted, "I had itchy feet," he had given her what would become her most famous song.

Friedman doubts that Janis could have ever settled down, even with Kristofferson, with whom she had much in common. While she loved to be in love, her drive to perform and her insatiable need to connect with the audience would probably have displaced even the most committed lover. As Janis herself told one interviewer, "Oh, hell, all any girl really wants is just love and a man. But what man can put up with a rock and roll star?"

In June 1970, Janis appeared on *The Dick Cavett Show* with Full-Tilt Boogie. Viewers saw a marked difference in her looks and demeanor from the lackluster 1969 appearance with Kozmic Blues, a visual metamorphosis of the stage persona she called Pearl. Pink feathers and a purple boa were woven into her hair and she wore a navy-and-purple rhinestone-encrusted pantsuit. She seemed more comfortable onstage when she performed "Move Over," encouraging the audience to join in clapping.

Afterward, a smiling Janis joined Cavett for an interview. Taking note of her breathlessness, Cavett asked if Janis got worn out from performing. She replied, "I get so turned on by doing one [song], it's hard to stop after doing one. It just makes you want to do more."

Cavett asked how she composed her songs. Janis replied, "I don't write songs; I just make 'em up."

When they chatted about Brazil, she commented that it was nice to take time off and to go relatively unnoticed, "just like a regular beatnik on the road."

Janis announced on the show that she was about to return to Port Arthur, Texas, for her tenth high school reunion. She playfully invited Cavett along as her date. Although he declined, saying he would hardly know anyone, he asked what she planned to do at the reunion.

"I'm gonna laugh a lot, man," Janis said, exuding confidence. She followed this statement with one that—though often repeated as a sign of her final struggles and deep sense of isolation—was most likely just jokey banter. "They laughed me out of the class, out of town and out of the state, man," she said. With a sly smile that was greeted with wild applause from the audience, she concluded, "So I'm going home."

Janis looked pleased with herself, and she may have truly felt pleased. Her career was at an all-time high, she was crazy about Full-Tilt Boogie, and she had a new love interest, Seth Morgan, the son of a wealthy East Coast family. She told one friend that Morgan treated her better than anyone ever had, making her feel more like a woman than any previous man. She even talked of marriage and about the potential for difficulty balancing a career with being a wife.

Friedman, suspecting Morgan was not the nice guy Janis believed him to be (Morgan would eventually serve time for armed robbery), worried about the relationship but trusted it would end quickly—as all Janis's romantic relationships had. Whatever Morgan's intentions, there wouldn't be time for them to play out.

On June 30, Janis joined other rock stars on a chartered train trip across Canada called the Festival Express, a weeklong party with performance stops along the way. Janis can be seen in film clips on the train, sitting with members of the Grateful Dead, comfortably in the center of things, often laughing, often drinking, sometimes chiming in on the chorus of a song. Always smiling.

9 Pearl

Janis returned to Texas in 1970 to sing at a birthday tribute to her old friend Ken Threadgill, the tavern owner who had opened his Austin Roadhouse to her and other singers back in the early 1960s. Janis tried to keep a low profile, not wanting to steal the limelight from Threadgill or the other performers. She finally took the stage, and as she picked up a guitar to accompany herself, she laughingly called out, "Gimme a git-tar. Whar's mah git-tar? Help. Help. I cain't tune it. Will someone tune this thing?" She performed two of Kris Kristofferson's songs, "Sunday Morning Coming Down" and "Me and Bobby McGee," to an enthusiastic crowd.

Then she was back on the road the next day with Full-Tilt Boogie, sharing the bill on two occasions with her original band, Big Brother and the Holding Company. It must have been bittersweet to see these close friends and yet not perform with them. Sam Andrew noticed that Janis's drinking was taking a toll; she looked red and puffy, and she'd gained weight.

OPPOSITE: This typical late-1960s concert hall lobby is decorated with antiwar and peace signs and invites protesters to gather petition signatures against the Vietnam War.

As her high school reunion loomed, Janis made another appearance on *The Dick Cavett Show*, on August 3. By now, her transformation into Pearl appeared complete. She had created a more glamorous version of herself, a public persona that could be bigger than life and that she may have hoped would protect her more private and vulnerable side.

She arrived in a rhinestone-encrusted suit and a silver vest. Her hair, which had taken on a russet shine, was woven with red boas. A bloodred heart-shaped choker worn on a red-beaded string hung around her neck like a talisman. When she sang, "Half Moon," followed by "My Baby," she projected complete confidence. She tossed her mane of hair and stomped and strutted.

After her performance, she and Cavett discussed the changing climate of the rock world and its effect on future rock concerts. Janis told a story of a cop clubbing a female fan who had tried to kiss her in Philadelphia. "And I didn't dig it," she said, referring to the police action. Janis felt the rock-and-roll industry would need to change, to take on some organization and a business structure, as its influence grew. She explained, "To have a really good festival, I think you have to have a lot of organizational ability and a lot of talent and a lot of bread to put things together so that it will even be functionable [*sic*] for the audiences let alone for the groups."

Janis was keenly aware that it was not only the rock climate that was changing. The year 1970 had witnessed frequent antiwar protests: Angry citizens had burned draft cards, stormed government buildings, and even burned the United States flag in objection to the Vietnam War, which had claimed tens of thousands of American lives. On August 6, Janis was one of a number of superstars who performed at the antiwar Peace Festival at Shea Stadium.

People who disliked rock music and the culture that surrounded it made stronger efforts to control and even close down concerts, which were growing more forceful and political in nature. A planned August 10 festival at Powder Ridge ski area in Connecticut was shut down by local authorities. When the biggest names in rock, including Janis, Joe Cocker, and Sly and the Family Stone, failed to arrive after their contracts were canceled, twenty thousand youths celebrated on their own, calling the week the "people festival." They created their own music, amplified by the power of two ice cream trucks. According to a *Time* editorial on the festival, there was such easy access to drugs that "kids on bad trips were treated by volunteer physicians, and were urged, over a makeshift public-address system to 'bring a few joints for the doctors.'"

It's easy to imagine that Janis would have loved Powder Ridge and gotten a huge kick out of the way the people rallied when the original plans for it fell through. But when her contract was canceled, Janis agreed to perform at Harvard Stadium on August 12 instead. No one could have imagined that this performance would be her last.

Janis returned to Port Arthur in August for her high school reunion, but it wasn't the laugh she'd anticipated. Despite a press conference and some attention from local media, Janis's classmates seemed mostly indifferent to her celebrity status. People failed to comment or fawn when she drove up in a limousine accompanied by an entourage that included musician Bobby Neuwirth; her road manager, John Byrne Cooke; and her sister, Laura. Few seemed fazed by the boas and beads, the round pink wire rims, and her satin outfit.

Time magazine summed up the low-key reaction when it reported that Janis won the prize for coming the longest distance: a flat tire. Fellow alums felt that, except for her wildly feathered and mod appearance, Janis hadn't really changed much. One classmate said kindly, "I hate to say she was a real lady because that's not her image. But she was."

Laura said, "Janis came home to get the accolades she didn't get in high school." But Laura doubted the reunion experience was as traumatic for Janis as some have speculated. She believed it gave her sister a sense of completion, a sense that she didn't "have to regret the original experiences anymore."

In September, Janis and Full-Tilt Boogie began studio sessions for *Pearl*. Throughout these sessions, the mood inside the studio was amiable. One day, as Janis prepared to sing "Me and Bobby McGee," a band member, possibly John Till, teased her about her Texas twang and she responded playfully, "Am I gettin' my Texas ac-cent back?" Janis's singing reflected her relaxed mood; she sounded warmer, less harsh, and more finely tuned. On a lark one day, she taped herself saying, "I have a message of great political importance," then sang, "Oh, Lo-rd, won't you buy me a Mercedes Benz." The tape caught her trademark giggle.

With this band and album, Janis had found her stride. More mature, she was able to tell her musicians exactly what she wanted of them, plus she genuinely liked them. They were talented and had become her good friends.

Janis didn't plan for *Pearl* to be her pinnacle. She intended to keep reaching creatively, to improve and

OPPOSITE: The cover of *Pearl* shows that the metamorphosis of Janis—with pink feathers in her hair, beaded necklaces, and bangles—into a celebrity was complete. She told an interviewer that the public persona of Pearl was borrowed from African American singer and actress Pearl Bailey, a star of stage, film, and television known for her warm comedic presense and colorful style.

OPPOSITE: The camera captures Janis preparing to belt out the blues at Woodstock.

experiment with her voice. In one of her last interviews, she was asked why she worked so hard. She responded that it "sure as hell" wasn't the money. "At first it was to get love from the audience. Now it's to reach my fullest potential, to go as far as I can go. I've got the chance. It's a great opportunity!" Sadly, Janis's demons lurked, waiting in the wings to pounce.

On the night of October 3, tired and alone after a full day in the studio, she listened to the instrumental track for the song "Buried Alive in the Blues." She was planning to record the vocals the next morning. The lyrics she rehearsed included the prophetic lines, "Bad luck pressing in from all sides / Buried alive in the blues."

Drunk in her room at the Landmark Motel, she popped a needle full of heroin just under her skin, went out to the lobby to buy herself a pack of cigarettes, and then returned to her room, where she sat down on her bed. A few moments later, shortly before two in the morning, the rock star slumped over, hitting her lip on the nightstand as she fell to the floor.

After Janis failed to show up at the recording studio the next morning, John Byrne Cooke drove to the Landmark, where he found her wedged between the bed and nightstand, dead from an accidental overdose of heroin mixed with alcohol.

There was not a big funeral. Only a small group, including her parents, gathered for a quiet seaside service. Her ashes, according to her wishes, were spread along Stinson Beach in Northern California over the Pacific Ocean. Janis Joplin was only twenty-seven years old.

OPPOSITE: This October 29, 1970, *Rolling Stone* cover mourns the loss of Janis Joplin, found dead in her hotel room on October 4 of that year.

ROLLING STONE

October 29, 1970
No. 69
UK: 3/-
50c

Janis Joplin

1943-1970

Jim Marshall

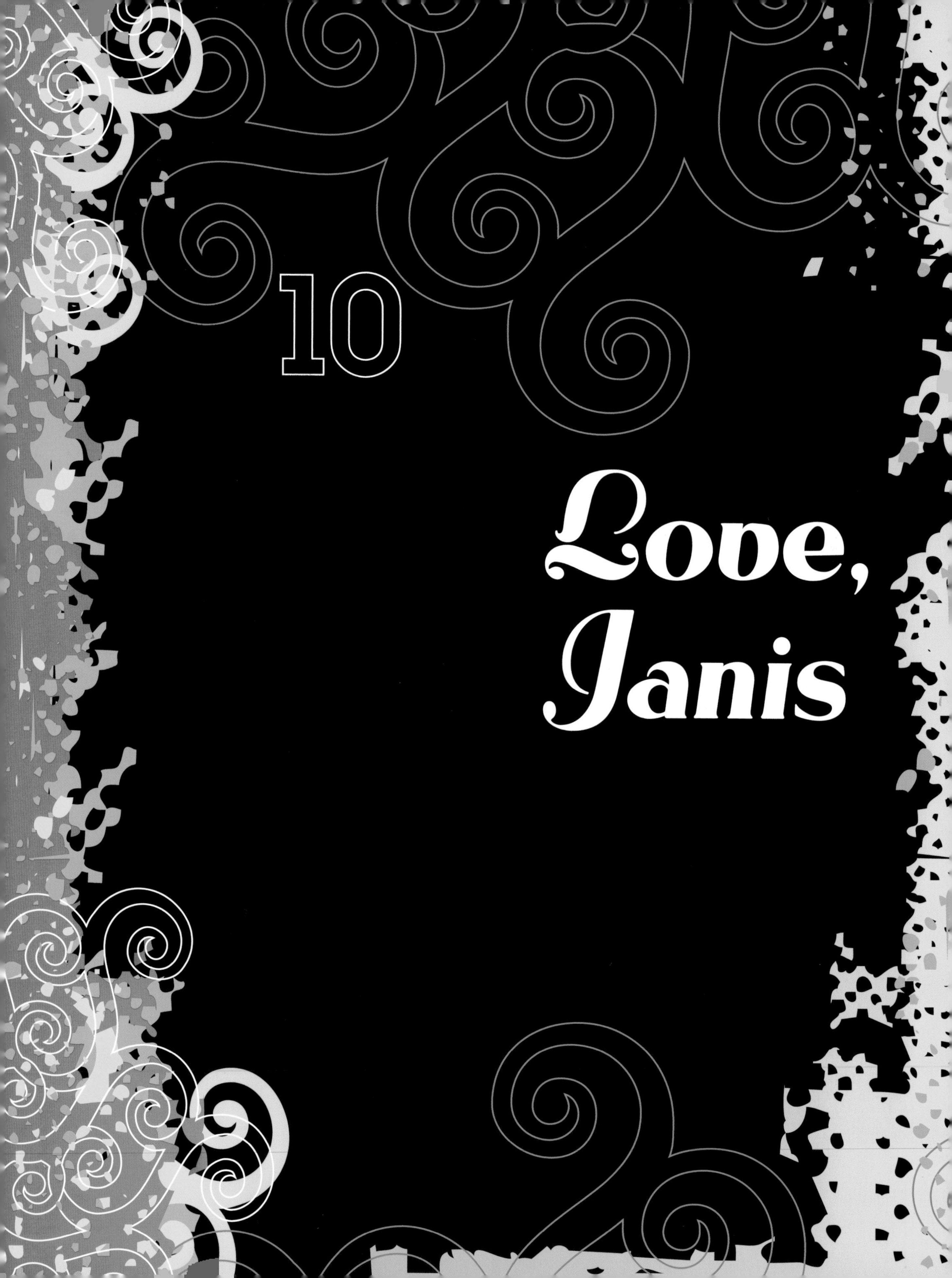

10

Love, Janis

Janis smiles during a publicity shoot.

After Janis's death, television host Dick Cavett said, "I think there were two Janises: There was the high school girl who desperately wanted acceptance and that character she created which was the tough-talking, tough-drugging, drinking rock and roll star."

Fame had nurtured and encouraged Janis's wild, over-the-top behavior. People loved when she swaggered onto the stage with a bottle of Southern Comfort or waxed lyrical about getting high. And, along the way, she became as hooked on adulation as she was on drugs and alcohol. It was the attention she had craved all her life, from her lonely high school days to her spirited college days to her crazy days in San Francisco, speeding around town in her psychedelic Porsche. To feed her voracious need for more love and praise, she became ever more outrageous. She took greater and greater personal risks until, finally, sheer carelessness caught up with her. As her obituary in *Time* magazine reported, she "died on the lowest and saddest of notes."

OPPOSITE: Six years after her death, Janis was honored by *Rolling Stone* as one of the top 100 rock and blues musicians.

When Myra Friedman first learned of Janis's death, she was angry, mainly at the culture of celebrity and drugs she felt had taken her friend away. Friedman had begged Janis to stop using heroin, and Janis had seemed to listen. "Janis trusted me more than anybody," said Friedman. "She was my friend. I really loved her." Though Janis would stop using for a while, she was perpetually surrounded by stoned groupies and hard-partying friends, and would soon give in to the impulse to shoot up again.

Janis's death, the direct result of her own recklessness, was simply an accident. For her family, many friends, and myriad fans, it was a profound, resounding tragedy and an incalculable loss.

Drummer Dave Getz said of Janis's death, "A lot of people say if she'd stayed with Big Brother, she'd still be alive or she wouldn't have lost her bearings. . . . [But] we had certain limitations. We couldn't be her ideal band."

Janis's talent was isolating. She was a woman lead singer in a time when men dominated the popular music scene. And she was a white woman who sang the blues, which was traditionally black music.

Time magazine concluded its obituary of Janis with the following: "Purists insist that no white man or woman can really sing the blues, because they cannot have known the pain of body and soul from which true blues rise. In her music, Janis certainly came as close to authentic blues as any white singer ever has." The article maintained that she defied the old-fashioned notion that race and art could not cross the color line, and that a white singer couldn't come close to reaching into the heart of the blues.

At the time of her death, Janis was earning more than any other female musician—a reported $50,000 a night. She proved that a woman could be a big draw for rock fans

SM14170

NOVEMBER 18th, 1976 • ISSUE NO. 226

85¢ UK50p

ROLLING STONE

JANIS

By Ellen Willis
A Special Preview of 'The Rolling Stone Illustrated History of Rock & Roll'

THE WAYWARD BUTZ

What He Really Said and What They Said He Said

Battle of the Bands:
THE WHO/DEAD SPREAD
By Annie Leibovitz

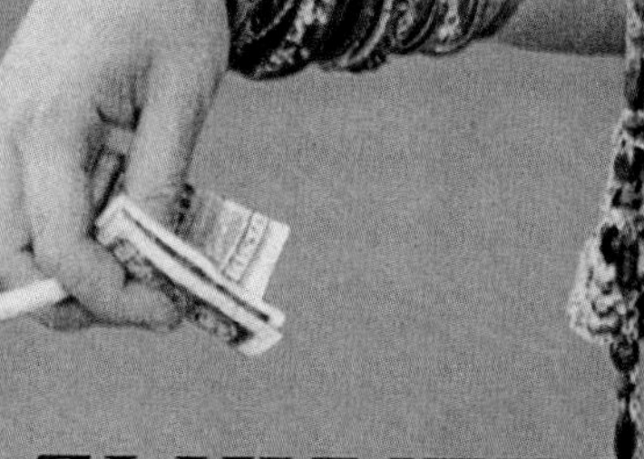

NAZI-HUNTING

By Greil Marcus

The Dreams and Dwarfs of Filmmaker
WERNER HERZOG
By Jonathan Cott

14023

and her boldly sexual, all-out style paved the way for future generations of female rockers and influenced countless performers, both male and female. Long after her death, Janis's name remains on top 100 lists of rock and blues musicians, and *Pearl* is a fixture on the *Rolling Stone* list of the 500 Greatest Albums of All Time. Testament to her boundless talent and energy, Janis's fans still can't get enough of her music. Even those who were too young to experience Janis's talent live are drawn to her mesmerizing performances, which seem to so perfectly capture the freedom and excitement of the time.

A stage play, *Love, Janis*, based on the book of the same name by Janis's sister Laura Joplin, features reenactments

Actress Cathy Richardson in costume as Janis to perform *Love, Janis.* Richardson believes that Janis carried a deep sadness within her that worked onstage but got the better of her offstage, also noting, "I found her, from her letters, to be ambitious, driven, extremely intelligent, funny and very wise for her age."

Laura Joplin's play about her sister, titled *Love, Janis,* after Laura's book of the same name, includes samples of the music Janis sang and snippets of letters she wrote home.

of some of the singer's iconic performances and excerpts from the many letters she wrote to her family. It's a revealing look at two very different sides of Janis: the wild, uninhibited performer and the sweet, solicitous daughter and sister.

Big Brother's Sam Andrew has worked as the music director of some of those productions. "It is like watching [*The*] *Twilight Zone* to see your life put on stage this way," he said. "Every night I see a different facet of our time together with Janis." One scene brings Janis to life for him every time: "When Janis says, in the play, that she is in a car and her arm is being jostled, so please excuse the handwriting, I always remember that I am the one who was next to her and bumped her arm. I saw many of those letters being written, and I can tell you that it is a bizarre experience to be standing in a theater thousands of miles away, and forty years later, hearing an actor talk about how her arm was disturbed and apologizing for the writing. If you had told Janis or me that this was going to happen in the twenty-first century, we would have laughed."

Janis was inducted into the Rock and Roll Hall of Fame on January 12, 1995. In November 2009, the Rock and Roll Hall of Fame and Museum hosted an "American Music Masters" tribute to Janis that featured Lucinda Williams performing a song she wrote for Janis. Country Joe McDonald and songwriter Bob Neuwirth, who wrote "Mercedes Benz," also performed.

Summing up Janis's influence, rock critic Lillian Roxon claimed, "[Janis Joplin] perfectly expressed the feelings and yearnings of the girls of the electric generation—to be all woman, yet equal with men; to be free, yet a slave to real love; to [reject] every outdated convention, and yet get back to the basics of life."

OPPOSITE: Melissa Etheridge (left) and Joss Stone perform the medley "Cry Baby/Piece of My Heart" in a tribute to Janis at the Forty-seventh Annual Grammy Awards, on February 13, 2005, at the Staples Center in Los Angeles. Etheridge's bald head is the result of her treatment for breast cancer.

OPPOSITE: An April 1969 photo of a smiling Janis with an Autoharp in London. Early in her career, she played the Autoharp and sang folk songs.

Sometimes Janis's amazing voice sings out—a startling surprise—from a radio or a friend's iPod. Her voice resonates with the blues of lost love, struggle, and exclusion. Yet as her voice cries those mournful notes and then reaches high in celebration, it continues to draw listeners into the spirit of freedom and unfettered emotion that defined a generation. Sometimes, all the love and passion of a lifetime can be found in a single voice raised in one heartbreaking song.

Time Line

January 19, 1943
- Janis Lyn Joplin born at St. Mary's Hospital, Port Arthur, Texas. Parents are Seth and Dorothy Joplin.

June 1960
- Graduates from Thomas Jefferson High School.

Fall 1960
- Attends Lamar Technical College.
- Visits Houston. Moves to Los Angeles and hangs out in Venice, California.

December 1961
- Returns to Port Arthur in a sheepskin jacket.

Fall 1962
- Enrolls at University of Texas, Austin. Nominated for "ugliest man on campus."
- Chet Helms, a former UT student, returns from San Francisco and tells her about the post-Beat scene.

January 23, 1963
- Hitches to San Francisco with Helms.
- Sings in North Beach, San Francisco, coffeehouses the Coffee and Confusion and the Coffee Gallery.

Summer 1963
- Involved in a motorscooter accident.

Summer 1964
- Lives in New York's Lower East Side. Shoots speed.

Fall 1964
- Returns to San Francisco.

May 1965
- So strung-out on speed that she attempts to get herself admitted to San Francisco General Hospital.
- Returns to Port Arthur. Registers in sociology at Lamar Tech.

Thanksgiving 1965
- Sings at the Half Way House in Beaumont.

Spring 1966
- Considers joining the band the Thirteenth Floor Elevators. Chet Helms recommends her as the "chick singer" to Big Brother and the Holding Company and sends Travis Rivers, Janis's old friend from Port Arthur, to persuade her.

July 1, 1966

- Moves to a house in Lagunitas in the San Geronimo Valley in Marin County with members of Big Brother and their wives and girlfriends.

August 5–6, 1966

- Plays at the Avalon Ballroom in San Francisco with Big Brother and Bo Diddley.

August–September, 1966

- Plays four weeks at Mother Blues, Chicago.
- Signs with Mainstream Records and records an album.

January 1, 1967

- New Year's Wail/Whale in Panhandle Park, San Francisco with the Grateful Dead.

January 14, 1967

- Performs at the first Be-In in Golden Gate Park, San Francisco, with the Grateful Dead and Jefferson Airplane.

February 5, 1967

- California Hall, San Francisco, with Blue Cheer: Hell's Angels benefit. Performances delayed while University of California law students finish bar exams.

February 10, 1967

- Meets Country Joe McDonald at the Golden Sheaf Bakery in Berkeley, California.

May 12–13, 1967

- Winterland Ballroom, San Francisco.

June 17–18, 1967

- Monterey International Pop Festival.

September 15, 1967

- The Hollywood Bowl.

November 1967

- Big Brother signs Albert Grossman as manager.
- The Fillmore West, San Francisco.

December 1967

- Goes home to Port Arthur for Christmas.

March 1, 1968

- Grande Ballroom in Detroit, filmed performance.

March–April 1968

- Cuts *Cheap Thrills* at Columbia's Studio E in New York.

April 1968

- *Cheap Thrills* sessions continue at Columbia's Hollywood studios.

April 11, 1968

- ABC-TV's *Hollywood Palace*.

June 1968

- Big Brother returns to NY for more recording sessions. Enough orders have been taken to ensure the album gold status.

August 1968

- Plays the Newport Folk Festival in Rhode Island. *Cheap Thrills* released, and sales exceed a million copies in the first month despite mixed reviews.

September 1968

- Split between Janis and Big Brother announced.

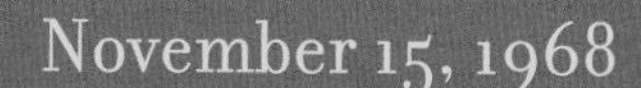

November 15, 1968

- Last East Coast performance with Big Brother at Hunter College, Manhattan.

November 20, 1968

- Begins to put together new band.

December 1, 1968

- Big Brother's final performance with the Family Dog in San Francisco.

December 21, 1968

- Kozmic Blues plays at the Stax-Volt "Yuletide Thing" in Memphis.

February 1, 1969

- *Rolling Stone* magazine review of Kosmic Blues by Stanley Booth is sympathetic but negative.

March 15, 1969

- *Rolling Stone* magazine cover story: "Janis: The Judy Garland of Rock?" by Paul Nelson.

March 18, 1969

- *The Ed Sullivan Show*

June 1969

- Recording sessions with Kozmic Blues at Columbia's Hollywood studios.

July 18, 1969

- First appearance on *The Dick Cavett Show*.

August 15–17, 1969

- Woodstock Music and Art Fair in Bethel, New York. Sam Andrew leaves Kozmic Blues.

September 20, 1969

- The Hollywood Bowl.

November 1969

- *I Got Dem Ol' Kozmic Blues Again Mama!* album released.

November 16, 1969

- Charged with using obscene language during concert in Tampa, Florida.

November 27, 1969

- Sings with Tina Turner at Rolling Stones concert, Madison Square Garden, New York.

December 1969

- Moves to house in Larkspur, California.

January 1970

- Kozmic Blues disbands.

February 1970

- Flies to Rio de Janeiro, Brazil, for Carnival. Plans to get off drugs and dry out.

March 28, 1970

- Records "One Night Stand" with Paul Butterfield in Hollywood.

April 1970

- Assembles third and final group, Full-Tilt Boogie. Falls for movie star and country singer Kris Kristofferson, who writes her the song "Me and Bobby McGee."

April 4, 1970

- Big Brother reunion at Fillmore West, San Francisco.

April 12, 1970

- Janis and Big Brother play the Winterland Ballroom, San Francisco.

May 1970

- Begins touring with Full-Tilt Boogie.

June 12–24, 1970

- Full-Tilt plays Freedom Hall, Louisville, Kentucky. Also plays Kansas City, Santa Ana, California, and San Bernardino, California.

June 25, 1970

- Appears on *The Dick Cavett Show* with Full-Tilt Boogie.

June 30–July 4, 1970

- The Festival Express tours across Canada.

July 10, 1970

- Sings at birthday celebration for Ken Threadgill, Austin, Texas.

July 11, 1970

- Full-Tilt and Big Brother share billing in San Diego.

August 3, 1970

- Appears on *The Dick Cavett Show* with her new persona, Pearl.

August 6, 1970

- Shea Stadium Peace Festival, New York.

August 12, 1970

- Harvard Stadium, Massachusetts—last concert.

August 14, 1970

- Attends high school reunion in Port Arthur, Texas.

September 1970

- *Pearl* sessions in Los Angeles, California.

October 3, 1970

- Final instrumental track for *Pearl*, "Buried Alive in the Blues" by Nick Gravenites, completed. Janis plans to record vocals the following day.

October 4, 1970

- Overdoses from a combination of heroin and alcohol in her room at the Landmark Hotel, Los Angeles, California.

January 12, 1995

- Inducted into the Rock and Roll Hall of Fame, Cleveland, Ohio.

April 22, 2001

- *Love, Janis*, a play based on Janis's letters home, debuts off-Broadway.

February 13, 2005

- Melissa Etheridge and Joss Stone perform a tribute to Janis at the 42nd Annual Grammy Awards.

November 14, 2009

- The American Music Masters Tribute to Janis Joplin. Lucinda Williams performs song about Janis.

Acknowledgments

This book took longer to develop than many rock stars' careers have survived, but it was worth every sweet and tormented moment. The idea first gelled when my friend Paula Graham insisted my short piece about my idol Janis Joplin was book worthy, but I shoved it into a drawer full of great, unfinished ideas. There it sat until I showed it to friends at the Vermont College of Fine Arts. They encouraged me, and two of my advisers, Chris Lynch and Graham "Sandy" Salisbury, jumped on the rock-star wagon and told me to make it happen.

My editor, Susan Van Metre, who fell in love with this project the first time I mentioned it, gets major gold stars from me as well as gratitude. I also wish to thank my agent, Barry Goldblatt, who worked to make this a reality. This biography of Janis could only be set in both historical and personal contexts because of the written memories of many, including Laura Joplin, Big Brother and the Holding Company, keepers of Janis's fan sites, and others. Through a flurry of e-mails from Janis's guitarist and friend, Sam Andrew, and her road manager, John Byrne Cooke, I discovered the enduring quality of friendship over time and tragedy. I will be forever indebted to Janis's publicist and friend, Myra Friedman. Over the last few years, our phone calls, which began as interviews, evolved into a warm friendship. Myra has a lovely way of speaking in italics about those she holds dear. She has said, "Janis was an amazing, *amazing* woman. I *adored* her." Myra, I *adore* you.

Thank you, dear early readers: Sharon Addy, Dori Chaconas, JoAnn Macken, Gretchen Mayo, and Lisa Moser. Thank you to my friend Heidi Sjostrom for taking on a final critical read, to my colleagues at Mount Mary College who encourage me always—you know who you are. It takes a virtual concert crew of publishing staff to make books happen, and so thank you to designer extraordinaire Maria T. Middleton, incredible marketing director Jason Wells, organizational genius Brett Wright, editor Susan Homer, and all those behind the scenes at Amulet, as well as to the photographers included on these pages for agreeing to license the images.

Again, to my editor, Susan Van Metre—this book would never have been born if not for you, and it might not have the emotional resonance it now bears if not for your gentle teasing when I tried to stiff-arm the heartbreak of Janis's life.

I also send my family gratitude for their faith that I could render this life lived without compromise to the page. Thank you to John and Mary Bonness and Jean Angel, who always asked how it was going, and to my brothers and sisters, Katie, Johnny, Jeannie, Peter, Barbie, Lorrie, and Joannie, who encourage me always even if it's by asking, "Aren't you finished with that book *yet*?" I love you and your significant others. To my immediate family: Jeff, Amanda, Nick, Joe, and Stevi, who proved stoic when I woke the house with Janis singing us into the decade with "Cry Baby." You not only accepted years of all things Janis, but embraced her with me. You're my rock stars now and always. Thank you.

Notes

CHAPTER 1

Page 5: "For a while, two boys followed her around . . . nigger lover." Myra Friedman, *Buried Alive, The Biography of Janis Joplin* (New York: Harmony Books/Random House, 1992), pp. 11–12.

Page 7: "The only people for me . . . mad to be saved." Jack Kerouac, quoted in "Jack Kerouac, *On the Road*," posted on the Quote Snack blog, http://www.quotesnack.com/jack-kerouac/the-only-people-for-me-are-the-mad-ones-the-ones-who-are-mad-to-live-mad-to-talk-mad-to-be-saved/.

Page 9: It made her want to . . . type. From "Port Arthur High School Reunion Lyrics," posted on the Web site Metro Lyrics, http://www.metrolyrics.com/port-arthur-high-school-reunion-lyrics-janis-joplin.html and http://www.harptab.com/lyrics/ly2468.shtml.

CHAPTER 2

Page 13: "She went to church . . . good as she wanted." Janis's father, quoted in "Interview with Janis's Father," with Chet Filippo, November 12, 1970, http://www.janisjoplin.net./articles/?id=z47.

Page 17: "We wanted them to voice their opinions . . . about everything." Janis's mother, Dorothy, quoted in *Buried Alive*, pp. 11–12.

Page 17: By the time she was seventeen . . . Rest. From *Buried Alive*, pp. 20–21.

Page 18: "Janis wouldn't accept the limits . . . own limits." Laura Joplin, *Love, Janis* (Petaluma, CA: Acid Test Productions, 1992), p. 68.

Page 18: He called it the "Saturday Night Swindle . . . worth the price." Janis's father, quoted in *Love, Janis* (Acid Test, 1992), p. 70.

Page 19: "anyone with ambition like me . . . put down." Janis, quoted on *20/20 Downtown*, ABC News, January 13, 2000.

Page 19: When they had a free day, . . . been drinking. From *Buried Alive*, 29.

CHAPTER 3

Page 21: Before her first semester ended . . . the college. From *Love, Janis* (New York: Harper, 2005), p. 83.

Page 22: Her parents agreed that she should look . . . and Mimi. From *Buried Alive*, pp. 26–27.

Page 22: Bored and restless, she longed to explore . . . ends meet. From *Buried Alive*, pp. 26–27.

Page 24: "Doesn't anybody . . . ball, man?" Janis, quoted in *Buried Alive*, p. 27.

Page 25: "I want to want the white house . . . but I just don't." Janis, quoted in *Love, Janis* (Acid Test, 1992), p. 86.

Page 26: "She goes barefooted when she feels like it . . . unrestrained." Pat Sharpe, "She Dares to Be Different," originally published in *The Daily Texan* (July 22, 1962), reprinted on the ZACH Theatre Web site, http://www.zachtheatre.org/blog/?tag=janis-joplin.

Page 26: "a certain spontaneity and gusto." "She Dares to be Different," http://www.zachtheatre.org/blog/?tag=janis-joplin.

Page 26: Shortly after, she wrote to her parents . . . so cruel. From *Love, Janis*, p. 98, and *Buried Alive*, pp. 40–41.

Page 28: In the years to come . . . with women. From *Buried Alive*, p. 35.

Page 28: "She had smoked a few joints . . . in Venice." Myra Friedman, *Buried Alive*, p. 39.

Page 29: After hearing Janis sing . . . San Francisco. From *Buried Alive*, pp. 39, 43–44.

Page 29: She returned to the Fox and Hound . . . for a gig. From "Any Port Arthur in a Storm," posted on David Archer's official Web site, http://www.davearcher.com/Joplin.html.

Page 30: Drunk, she hurt her leg . . . to have. From "Chronology," posted on a Janis fan site, http://www.janisjoplin.net.

Page 30: "The longer [Janis] stayed in California . . . she sought." Laura Joplin, *Love, Janis* (Acid Test, 1992), p. 124.

Page 31: "Life looked . . . more creative." Laura Joplin, *Love, Janis* (Acid Test, 1992), p.127.

Page 31: She left San Francisco in May 1965 . . . her wedding. From *Love, Janis* (Acid Test, 1992), pp. 126–30.

Page 32: "My parents . . . holding their breath." Laura Joplin, in "Talkback," a post-show discussion of her play, St. Paul's Ordway Center for the Performing Arts, March 8, 2007.

Page 32: Deep down, she wanted . . . to love her. From *Buried Alive*, pp. 67–68.

Page 32: "something interesting to . . . happen." Laura Joplin, *Love, Janis* (Acid Test, 1992), p. 138.

Page 33: "the best blues singer in the country." Janis's friend Jim Langdon, quoted in *Love, Janis* (Acid Test, 1992), pp. 138–41.

Page 33: Before long, singing offers came . . . to music. From *Love, Janis* (Acid Test, 1992), pp. 138–41.

Page 33: "You wanted to say . . . the sociologist.'" Myra Friedman, from a telephone interview with Ann Angel, June 18, 2008.

CHAPTER 4

Page 37: "Few were then questioning . . . new shaman?" Laura Joplin, *Love, Janis*, (Acid Test, 1992), p. 165.

Page 37: "a singer who could . . . instrumental energies." Sam Andrew, "Janis First Person," http://www.bbhc.com/Janis_First_Person.html.

Page 38: "whether you liked her or not . . . a phenomenon." Dave Getz, quoted on the album *Big Brother and the Holding Company with Janis Joplin: Nine Hundred Nights* (Cheap Thrills Music, 2004).

Page 38: "progressive regressive hurricane blues." Sam Andrew, "History, Band," posted on the Big Brother Holding Company official Web site, http://www.bbhc.com.

Page 38: "The music was boom, boom, boom . . . boys.'" Janis, quoted in Alice Echols, *Scars of Sweet Paradise* (New York: Henry Holt and Company, 1999), p. 134.

Page 38: Rough and raucous, the results . . . screaming. From *Scars of Sweet Paradise*, p. 134.

Page 38: "lose the chick." From *Nine Hundred Nights*, 2004.

Page 42: To work on unifying . . . and songwriting. From "History, Band," http://www.bbhc.com.

Page 42: "It was totally furnished . . .Victorian fru fru . . ." Joe McDonald, "Janis Joplin," http://www.countryjoe.com/autobio.htm.

Page 42: "scream and yell and screech." Joe McDonald, quoted in *Buried Alive*, p. 81.

Page 45: Janis blended her own gravelly blues . . . crooned ballads. From AOL Music, http://music.aol.com/artist/otis-redding/biography/1004516.

Page 45: "I do believe ... in the air." Janis, quoted in *Love, Janis* (Acid Test, 1992), p. 232.

Page 45: While Janis was already a spectacular, larger-than-life presence . . . acid riffs. From *Scars of Sweet Paradise*, pp. 153–55.

CHAPTER 5

Page 47: The highlight of the year was the Summer of Love. From an article by Erika Cox, posted on the Web site Rewind the Fifties, http://www.loti.com/sixties_music/Monterey_Pop_Festival_1967.htm.

Page 48: "the summer of free love and rock and roll." John Phillips, audio interview, *The Complete Monterey Pop Festival* (CA: The Monterey Pop Festival Foundation, Inc. and Pennebaker-Hegedus Films, Inc., 2002).

Page 48: "Oh, oh, o-oo-wowo-waha . . . go wrong?" Janis, quoted in Lou Adler and John Phillips, audio commentary and interview, *The Complete Monterey Pop Festival*, 2002.

Pages 48–49: "Oh people, it ain't fair what you do." Janis, quoted in *The Complete Monterey Pop Festival*, 2002.

Page 49: "Everybody . . . down on me." Janis, quoted in *The Complete Monterey Pop Festival*, 2002.

Page 49: "Wow!" Cass Elliot, quoted in *The Complete Monterey Pop Festival*, 2002.

Page 51: "brought the house down . . . magnificent voice." A *Rolling Stone* critic, quoted in *Nine Hundred Nights*, 2004.

Page 52: "I thought it was Tic Tacs . . . many of them." Sam Andrew, quoted in *Nine Hundred Nights*, 2004.

Pages 52–53: "[Janis] was skipping around . . . nude." Laura Joplin, "Talkback," March 8, 2007.

Page 53: "Isn't it wonderful? . . . you see?" Janis, quoted in *Love, Janis* (Harper, 2005), p. 204.

Page 53: "rich in detail . . . experiencing." Laura Joplin, "Talkback," March 8, 2007.

Page 53: "All have their hair . . . Beatle length." Janis, quoted in *Love, Janis* (Acid Test, 1992), p. 158.

Page 55: While touring with the band . . . concerts. From *Buried Alive*, p. 210.

Page 57: "But for awhile, there were . . . difference." Janis, quoted in *Love, Janis* (Acid Test, 1992), p. 158.

Page 57: Columbia Records . . . music companies. From *Nine Hundred Nights*, 2004.

Page 57: "We felt we had a fabulous weapon . . . band." Dave Getz, quoted in *Nine Hundred Nights*, 2004.

Page 57: "There was something wrong . . . movie." Dave Getz, quoted in *Nine Hundred Nights*, 2004.

Page 57: Myra Friedman, the band's new publicist . . . album. From Myra Friedman's telephone interview with Ann Angel, January 4, 2010.

Page 58: "possibly the best . . . her generation." *Rolling Stone* magazine, cited in *Love, Janis* (Harper, 2005), p. 213.

Page 58: "The plumage and the punch . . . is over." The *Village Voice*, cited in *Love, Janis* (Harper, 2005), p. 213.

Page 58: "Do I look old?" Janis, quoted in Friedman, telephone interview, June 18, 2008.

Page 59: Beforehand, however, he made a telling change . . . "featuring Janis Joplin." Laura Joplin, *Love, Janis* (Acid Test, 1992), p. 220.

Page 59: "Twenty-five. 25 . . . this long." Janis, quoted in *Love, Janis* (Acid Test, 1992), p. 221.

CHAPTER 6

Page 61: "Purple Haze" . . . half the year. From *Billboard*, http://www.billboard.com/bbcom/bio/index.jsp?pid=69498.

Page 61: Jefferson Airplane . . . certified gold. From *Billboard*, http://www.billboard.com/bbcom/bio/index.jsp?pid=4927.

Page 61: The Grateful Dead . . . live performances. From *Billboard*, http://www.billboard.com/bbcom/bio/index.jsp?pid=4743.

Page 61: pressure . . . commercial format. From *Nine Hundred Nights*, 2004.

Page 62: "I ain't singing with those . . . motherfuckers!" Janis, quoted in *Love, Janis* (Acid Test, 1992), p. 224, and *Buried Alive*, p. 119.

Page 62: "Hush little baby . . . cryyyyyyy." Janis, quoted in *Nine Hundred Nights*, 2004.

Page 63: "Even then . . . for the better." John Byrne Cooke, e-mail to Ann Angel, December 3, 2007.

Page 64: "Big Brother is just a wretched . . . at all." Michael Bloomfield, quoted in *Scars of Sweet Paradise*, p. 212.

Pages 64–65: "I had the chick in my manager's office . . . two years." Janis, quoted in *Love, Janis* (Acid Test, 1992), p. 259.

Page 65: The company . . . as thanks. From *Buried Alive*, p. 135

Page 65: "[Janis] said it was the blues-singer . . . messed up." A friend of Janis, quoted in *Love, Janis* (Acid Test, 1992), p. 233.

Page 65: "When I go onstage to sing . . . any more." Janis, quoted in "Passionate and Sloppy," *Time*, August 9, 1968.

Page 65: "Performing with Janis was an adrenaline-raising . . . out." James Gurley, quoted in *Love, Janis* (Harper, 2005), pp. 278–79.

Page 65: "Janis was no longer . . . her." Laura Joplin, *Love, Janis* (Harper, 2005), p. 280.

Page 67: Pre-sale orders were off the charts . . . available. From "Chronology," http://www.janisjoplin.net.

Page 67: "It was too late . . . no surprise." Dave Getz, quoted in *Nine Hundred Nights*, 2004.

Page 67: "I love those guys more than . . . leave." Janis, quoted in *Scars of Sweet Paradise*, p. 215.

Page 67: After that, manager Albert Grossman . . . move on. From "Chronology," http://www.janisjoplin.net.

CHAPTER 7

Page 69: The problem wasn't just that the heady mix. From *Buried Alive*, p. 163.

Page 70: Although critics praised . . . less than thrilled. From *Buried Alive*, pp. 144–61.

Page 71: "A number of musicians were there . . . job." Myra Friedman, *Buried Alive*, p. 152.

Page 71: Reviews such as Ralph J. Gleason's . . . stung. From "Chronology," http://www.janisjoplin.net.

Page 71: "I'm gonna try . . . lose you." Janis, from "Janis Joplin Try [Live] w/ Kozmic Blues Band," posted on YouTube, http://www.youtube.com/watch?v=KnEUXKb7LpI&feature=related.

Pages: 71, 74–75: Upon their return to the United States on July . . . emotion of it. From *The Dick Cavett Show: Rock Icons*, produced by Judith Englander (Los Angeles: Daphne Productions, 2005), Disk 2.

Page 75: "Yeah, I know I might be going . . . watching TV." Janis, quoted in "Every Moment Site Is What She Feels: The Janis Joplin Philosophy," Michael Lyden, *New York Times Magazine*, February 23, 1969, p. SM36.

Page 75: "She was brilliant . . . well read." Myra Friedman, telephone interview, June 18, 2008.

Page 75: She performed more than a hundred . . . memorabilia. From "Chronology," http://www.janisjoplin.net/life/chronology/.

Page 76: "We don't need a leader . . . to live." Janis, quoted in "The Message of History's Biggest Happening," *Time*, August 29, 1969.

Page 78: "I don't mind getting arrested . . . kids on." Janis, quoted in "People," *Time*, November 28, 1969.

Page 78: The temporary affection . . . loneliness. From *Buried Alive*, p. 151.

Page 78: "She saw her choice as either . . . status." Laura Joplin, *Love, Janis* (Harper, 2005), pp. 316–17.

CHAPTER 8

Page 81: "Janis Joplin has a set in satin." *Time* reporter, "The Psychedelic Tie-Dye Look," *Time*, January 26, 1970.

Page 81: "It's turning into a palace . . . FANTASTIC!" Janis, quoted in *Love, Janis* (Harper, 2005), p. 331.

Page 82: But Janis knew the group . . . 1970. From "Chronology," http://www.janisjoplin.net.

Page 82: Worn out, Janis made . . . Carnival. From *Scars of Sweet Paradise*, p. 271.

Page 82: Janis let her upset . . . use drugs again. From *Buried Alive*, p. 219.

Page 82: "I met a really fine man in Rio . . . now!" Janis, quoted in *Love, Janis* (Harper, 2005), p. 331.

Page 84: John Byrne Cooke remained as road manager . . . her voice. From "Chronology," http://www.janisjoplin.net.

Page 84: "I had itchy feet." Country singer Kris Kristofferson, quoted in *Buried Alive*, p. 203.

Page 84: While she loved to be in love . . . lover. From Friedman's telephone interview with Ann Angel, January 4, 2010.

Page 84: "Oh, hell, all any girl . . . star?" Janis, quoted in *Love, Janis* (Harper, 2005), pp. 367–68.

Page 86: "They laughed me out of class . . . going home." Janis, quoted in *The Dick Cavett Show*, 2005.

Page 87: She even talked of marriage . . . a wife. From *Buried Alive*, p. 203.

Page 87: On June 30, Janis joined other rock . . . way." From "Chronology," http://www.janisjoplin.net.

CHAPTER 9

Page 89: She performed two of Kris Kristofferson's songs . . . crowd. From "Life: Kenneth Threadgill," posted on a Janis fan site, http://www.janisjoplin.net/life/friends/kenneth-threadgill/.

Page 89: Sam Andrew noticed that Janis's . . . weight. From *Love, Janis* (Acid Test, 1992), p. 289.

Page 90: She tossed her mane of hair . . . and strutted. From *The Dick Cavett Show*, 2005.

Page 90: "To have a really good festival . . . groups." Janis, quoted in *The Dick Cavett Show*, 2005.

Page 90: Janis was one of a number of . . . Shea Stadium. From "Chronology," http://www.janisjoplin.net.

Page 91: "kids on bad trips . . . doctors.'" "Youth: Peace and Pot on Powder Ridge," *Time*, August 10, 1970.

Page: 92: No one could have imagined . . . last. From *Buried Alive*, p. 122.

Page 93: "I hate to say she was a real lady . . . she was." A former Port Arthur classmate, quoted in *Time*, August 10, 1970.

Page 93: "Janis came home to get . . . school." Laura Joplin, "Talkback," 2008.

Page 93: "have to regret . . . anymore." Laura Joplin, "Talkback," 2008.

Page 93: In September, Janis and Full-Tilt Boogie . . . *Pearl*. From "Chronology," http://www.janisjoplin.net.

Page 93: "Am I gettin' my Texas . . . back?" Janis, quoted in "RARE First Studio Recording of 'Me and Bobby McGee,'" posted onYouTube, http://www.youtube.com/watch?v=irU5oihACj4.

Page 93: "Oh Lo-rd, won't . . . Mercedes Benz." Janis Joplin, *Pearl* (Columbia Records, 1971).

Page 94: "At first it was to get love from . . . opportunity!" Janis, quoted in *Love, Janis* (Harper, 2005), p. 352.

Page 94: She was planning to record . . . morning. From "Chronology," http://www.janisjoplin.net.

Page 94: "Bad luck pressing in . . . blues." Janis, quoted in "Joplin's Shooting Star," posted on The Pop History Dig Web site, http://www.pophistorydig.com/?tag=janis-joplin-high-school-reunion.

Page 94: A few moments later . . . floor. From *Buried Alive*, pp. 319-20.

Page 94: Her ashes, according to her wishes . . . Pacific Ocean. From *Buried Alive*, p. 322.

CHAPTER 10

Page 99: "I think there were two Janises . . . star." Dick Cavett, quoted in *20/20 Downtown*, January 13, 2000.

Page 99: "died on the lowest . . . notes." *Time* obituary, "Blues for Janis," October 19, 1970.

Page 100: "Janis trusted me more . . . loved her." Myra Friedman, telephone interview, January 4, 2010.

Page 100: "A lot of people . . . ideal band." David Getz, quoted in *Nine Hundred Nights*, 2004.

Page 100: "Purists insist . . . ever has." *Time* obituary, "Blues for Janis," October 19, 1970.

Page 102: *Pearl* is a fixture on the *Rolling Stone* . . . All Time. *Rolling Stone* magazine, http://www.rollingstone.com/news/story/5938174/the_rs_500_greatest_albums_of_all_time/2.

Page 102: "I found her . . . wise for her age." Cathy Richardson, e-mail to Ann Angel, January 9, 2008.

Page 105: "It is like watching . . . we would have laughed." Sam Andrew, e-mail to Ann Angel, January 17, 2008.

Page 105: "[Janis Joplin] perfectly expressed. . . basics of life." Lillian Roxon, quoted in "Janis Joplin Biography," posted on the Rock and Roll Hall of Fame and Museum official Web site, http://rockhall.com/inductees/janis-joplin/bio/.

Bibliography

AOL Music. "Otis Redding Biography." http://music.aol.com/artist/otis-redding/biography/1004516.

Big Brother and the Holding Company's official Web site. "Janis First Person." Sam Andrew. http://bbhc.com/Janis_First_Person.html.

Big Brother and the Holding Company with Janis Joplin: Nine Hundred Nights. LLC. Directed by Michael Burlingame. Cheap Thrills Music, 2004.

Billboard. http://www.billboard.com/bbcom/bio/index.jsp?pid=69498 (Jimi Hendrix page); http://www.billboard.com/bbcom/bio/index.jsp?pid=4927 (Jefferson Airplane page); and http://www.billboard.com/bbcom/bio/index.jsp?pid=4743 (Grateful Dead page).

"Blues for Janis." *Time*, October 19, 1970.

"Chronology." http://www.janisjoplin.net.

The Complete Monterey Pop Festival. DVD. Directed by Chris Hegedus and D. A. Pennebaker. With audio commentary by Lou Adler and an audio interview by John Phillips. CA: The Monterey Pop Festival Foundation, Inc. and Pennebaker-Hegedus Films, Inc., 2002.

Cooke, John Byrne. E-mail to Ann Angel, December 3, 2007.

Country Joe McDonald's official Web site. "Janis Joplin." Country Joe's Place. http://www.countryjoe.com/autobio.htm.

Cox, Erika. "The Monterey Pop Festival of 1967." Rewind the Fifties. http://www.loti.com/sixties_music/Monterey_Pop_Festival_1967.htm.

David Archer's official Web site. "Any Port Arthur in a Storm." David Archer. http://www.davearcher.com/Joplin.html.

The Dick Cavett Show: Rock Icons. DVD. Produced by Judith Englander. Los Angeles, CA: Daphne Productions, 2005.

Echols, Alice. *Scars of Sweet Paradise*. New York: Henry Holt and Company, 1999.

Friedman, Myra. *Buried Alive: The Biography of Janis Joplin*. New York: Harmony Books/Random House, 1992.

Friedman, Myra. Telephone interviews with Ann Angel, June 18, 2008 and January 4, 2010.

Janis Joplin fan site. "Interview with Janis's Father." By Chet Filippo. November 12, 1970. http://www.janisjoplin.net./articles/?id=z47.

——."Life: Kenneth Threadgill." http://www.janisjoplin.net/life/friends/kenneth-threadgill/.

Joplin, Janis. *Pearl*. Columbia Records, 1971.

Joplin, Janis. "Port Arthur High School Reunion Lyrics." Metro Lyrics: Beyond the Words, MetroLeap Media, Inc. http://www.metrolyrics.com/port-arthur-high-school-reunion-lyrics-janis-joplin.html.

Joplin, Laura. *Love, Janis*. Petaluma, CA: Acid Test Productions, 1992.

Joplin, Laura. *Love, Janis*. New York: Harper, 2005.

Joplin, Laura. "Talkback," *Love, Janis*. Ordway Theatre, 2008.

Lyden, Michael. "Every Moment Site Is What She Feels: The Janis Joplin Philosophy." *New York Times Magazine*, Sunday, February 23, 1969, p. 36.

"The Message of History's Biggest Happening." *Time*, August 29, 1969.

"Passionate and Sloppy." *Time*. August 9, 1968.

"People," *Time*. November 28, 1969.

The Pop History Dig Web site. "Joplin's Shooting Star." The Pop History Dig. http:// www.pophistorydig.com/?tag=janis-joplin-high-school-reunion.

"The Psychedelic Tie-Dye Look." *Time*, January 26, 1970.

Quote Snack blog. "Jack Kerouac, *On the Road*." Quotesnack.com. http://www.quotesnack.com/jack-kerouac/the-only-people-for-me-are-the-mad-ones-the-ones-who-are-mad-to-live-mad-to-talk-mad-to-be-saved/.

Richardson, Cathy. E-mail to Ann Angel, January 9, 2008.

Rock and Roll Hall of Fame and Museum official Web site. "Janis Joplin: Inducted 1995." Rock and Roll Hall of Fame and Museum. http://www.rockhall.com/inductee/janis-joplin/.

——."A Look at the 14th Annual AMM Tribute Concert from the Rock Hall's Vice President of Education." Dr. Lauren Onkey. http://rockhall.com/blog/post/1166_14th-annual-amm-tribute/.

Sharpe, Pat. "She Dares to Be Different." *The Daily Texan*, Friday, July 22, 1962. Reprinted on ZACH Theatre Web site. http://www.zachtheatre.org/blog/?tag=janis-joplin.

Siegel, Joel. "20/20 Downtown." ABC News, January 13, 2000.

"Youth: Peace and Pot on Powder Ridge." *Time*, August 10, 1970.

YouTube. "Janis Joplin Try [Live] w/ Kozmic Blues Band." XtinaxFan. http://www.youtube.com/watch?v=KnEUXKb7LpI&feature=related.

——."RARE First Studio Recording of 'Me and Bobby McGee.' XtinaxFan. http://www.youtube.com/watch?v=irU5oihACj4.

Image Credits

Jacket front (top), jacket back, pages 49, 54, 77, 99, 107: John Byrne Cooke. **Jacket front (bottom left and right), front and back cover, half-title page, pages 72, 73, 74, 91:** Amalie R. Rothschild. **Pages ii, 11, 66:** The Smithsonian Folkways Music/Ralph Rinzler Folklife Archives and Collections. **Pages vi, 52, 69, 103:** Sam Andrew. **Pages 1, 2, 3, 8:** Port Arthur Public Library. **Pages 4, 5, 8, 11, 13, 35, 36, 47:** AP Images/Photographer. **Page 6:** AP Images/Twardowicz. **Pages 7, 14, 15, 16, 23, 55:** Museum of the Gulf Coast. **Page 25:** AP Images/LM Otero. **Page 27:** Briscoe Center for American History, Cactus Yearbook. **Pages 29, 59, 95:** Don Aters. **Pages 39, 43, 44:** Family Dog. **Pages 40, 41, 56:** Lisa Law. **Pages 50, 79, 83, 97, 101:** Wenner Media, LLC. **Pages 51, 63, 70, 92, 103:** Sony. **Page 85:** Robert Altman. **Page 104:** AP Images/Kevork Djansezian.

Index

Page numbers in italics refer to illustrations.

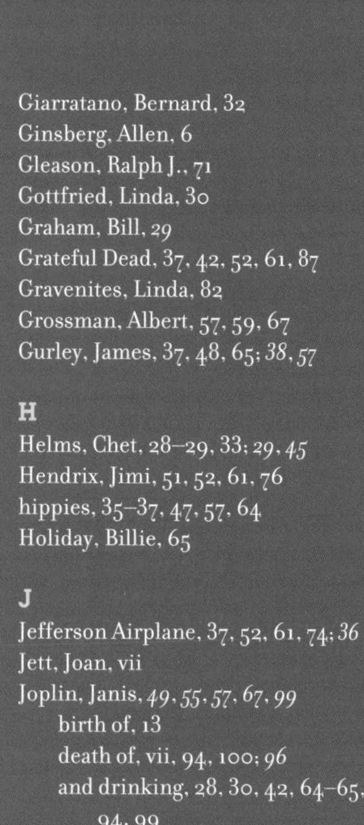